10641179

PRAISE FOR
RUTHLESS EXECUTION

"Based on my experience with companies over the last few years *Ruthless Execution* is a very timely book. Amir Hartman provides business leaders with a concise and well-reasoned set of guidelines to get their companies through performance downturns and prepared to exploit an economic recovery."

—JAMES I. CASH, PH.D.,
JAMES E. ROBISON PROFESSOR OF BUSINESS ADMINISTRATION,
HARVARD BUSINESS SCHOOL,
MEMBER OF THE BOARD—
CHUBB, GE, MICROSOFT, SCIENTIFIC ATLANTA

"Hartman delivers no-nonsense principles that hit at the essence of what it takes to break through the wall. The book offers a roadmap that business leaders would do well to follow."

—RUSS MCMEEKIN,
CEO, MIKOHN

"Loud and clear! Hartman effectively demonstrates what business practices work in tough times, and in my opinion these are practices that should be part of the business leader's DNA."

—VIJAY GOVINDARAJAN,
EARL C. DAUM PROFESSOR OF INTERNATIONAL BUSINESS,
AND DIRECTOR, CENTER FOR GLOBAL LEADERSHIP,
TUCK SCHOOL OF BUSINESS, DARTMOUTH COLLEGE

"Having the opportunity to lead a company that Hit the Wall, I have personally experienced the leadership challenges Hartman's latest book so clearly articulates. His examples and insights are real, his conclusions are accurate, and his roadmap and compelling arguments for *Ruthless Execution* work."

—BRUCE NELSON,
CHAIRMAN AND CEO,
OFFICE DEPOT

"Hartman does it again. *Ruthless Execution* is easy to read, easy to follow, and a must read for serious business leaders."

—LARRY KITTELBERGER,
SVP ADMINISTRATION AND CIO,
HONEYWELL INTERNATIONAL

"Pragmatic and a great read. *Ruthless Execution* gives business leaders insightful and to the point principles for overcoming performance plateaus."

—JEFF STEIN,
DEPUTY CHAIRMAN & COO, KPMG

"The messages are clear and powerful. Smart business leaders need to focus on what matters and drive accountability. Hartman shows us how to do this."

—VERNON ALTMAN,
DIRECTOR, BAIN & COMPANY

"In today's tough business environment, a new leadership paradigm is emerging—a call to action that compels today's leaders to take stock, face reality, act quickly and implement ruthlessly. Leaders today must be proactive, ambitious, focused and, above all, personally accountable. I applaud Hartman's book for tackling this issue head on. *Ruthless Execution* is a must read for leaders in all industries."

—STEVE LORANGER,
EXECUTIVE VICE PRESIDENT & COO,
TEXTRON

"A powerful book. Hartman does not let you off the hook until you think about where your business stands and what change is needed to revitalize the organization."

STEPHEN LUCZO,
CHAIRMAN AND CEO, SEAGATE TECHNOLOGY

"Waiting is not a strategy. In this powerful and practical book, based on shoulder-to-shoulder experience with business leaders who've been there, Hartman outlines concrete plans for getting beyond planning to "ruthless execution." He's done the practice of management a great service: frameworks for thinking, checklists, a step-by-step approach. A must read for all of us navigating today's turbulent markets."

RALPH A. OLIVA, EXECUTIVE DIRECTOR,
INSTITUTE FOR THE STUDY OF BUSINESS MARKETS (ISBM),
SMEAL COLLEGE OF BUSINESS, PENN STATE UNIVERSITY

RUTHLESS EXECUTION

WHAT BUSINESS LEADERS DO WHEN THEIR COMPANIES HIT THE WALL

In an increasingly competitive world, it is quality
of thinking that gives an edge—an idea that opens new
doors, a technique that solves a problem, or an insight
that simply helps make sense of it all.

We work with leading authors in the various arenas
of business and finance to bring cutting-edge thinking
and best learning practice to a global market.

It is our goal to create world-class print publications
and electronic products that give readers
knowledge and understanding which can then be
applied, whether studying or at work.

To find out more about our business
products, you can visit us at www.ft-ph.com

RUTHLESS EXECUTION

WHAT BUSINESS LEADERS DO WHEN THEIR COMPANIES HIT THE WALL

AMIR HARTMAN

FINANCIAL TIMES

An Imprint of PEARSON EDUCATION
Upper Saddle River, NJ • New York • London • San Francisco • Toronto • Sydney
Tokyo • Singapore • Hong Kong • Cape Town • Madrid
Paris • Milan • Munich • Amsterdam

www.ft-ph.com

Library of Congress Cataloging-in-Publication Data

Hartman, Amir.
  Ruthless execution : what business leaders do when their companies hit the wall / Amir Hartman.
    p. cm.
  Includes index.
  ISBN 0-13-101884-1
    1. Corporate turnarounds--Management. 2. Leadership. 3. Strategic panning. 4. Governance. 5. Executive ability. I. Title.

  HD58.8H3685 2004
  658.4'063--dc21   2003053154

Editor-in-chief: *Timothy C. Moore*
Editorial assistant: *Richard Winkler*
Development editor: *Russ Hall*
Editorial/production supervision: *Donna Cullen-Dolce*
Manufacturing buyer: *Maura Zaldivar*
Cover design director: *Jerry Votta*
Cover design: *Nina Scuderi*
Art Director: *Gail Cocker-Bogusz*
Interior Design: *Meg Van Arsdale*

© 2004 by Pearson Education, Inc.
Publishing as Financial Times Prentice Hall
Upper Saddle River, New Jersey 07458

Financial Times Prentice Hall offers excellent discounts on this book when ordered in quantity for bulk purchases or special sales. For more information, please contact U.S. Corporate and Government Sales: 1- 800-382-3419, or corpsales@pearsontechgroup.com. For sales outside the United States, please contact International Sales: 1-317-581-3793, international@pearsonetechgroup.com

Any company and product names mentioned herein are the trademarks or registered trademarks of their respective owners.

All rights reserved. No part of this book may be reproduced, in any form or by any means, without permission in writing from the publisher.

Printed in the United States of America

5th Printing

ISBN 0-13-101884-1

Pearson Education LTD.
Pearson Education Australia PTY, Limited
Pearson Education Singapore, Pte. Ltd.
Pearson Education North Asia Ltd.
Pearson Education Canada, Ltd.
Pearson Educación de Mexico, S.A. de C.V.
Pearson Education—Japan
Pearson Education Malaysia, Pte. Ltd.

FINANCIAL TIMES PRENTICE HALL BOOKS

For more information, please go to www.ft-ph.com

Business and Technology

Sarv Devaraj and Rajiv Kohli
The IT Payoff: Measuring the Business Value of Information Technology Investments

Nicholas D. Evans
Business Innovation and Disruptive Technology: Harnessing the Power of Breakthrough Technology…for Competitive Advantage

Nicholas D. Evans
Consumer Gadgets: 50 Ways to Have Fun and Simplify Your Life with Today's Technology…and Tomorrow's

Faisal Hoque
The Alignment Effect: How to Get Real Business Value Out of Technology

Economics

David Dranove
What's Your Life Worth? Health Care Rationing…Who Lives? Who Dies? Who Decides?

John C. Edmunds
Brave New Wealthy World: Winning the Struggle for World Prosperity

Jonathan Wight
Saving Adam Smith: A Tale of Wealth, Transformation, and Virtue

Entrepreneurship

Oren Fuerst and Uri Geiger
From Concept to Wall Street: A Complete Guide to Entrepreneurship and Venture Capital

David Gladstone and Laura Gladstone
Venture Capital Handbook: An Entrepreneur's Guide to Raising Venture Capital, Revised and Updated

Erica Orloff and Kathy Levinson, Ph.D.
The 60-Second Commute: A Guide to Your 24/7 Home Office Life

Jeff Saperstein and Daniel Rouach
Creating Regional Wealth in the Innovation Economy: Models, Perspectives, and Best Practices

Finance

Aswath Damodaran
The Dark Side of Valuation: Valuing Old Tech, New Tech, and New Economy Companies

Kenneth R. Ferris and Barbara S. Pécherot Petitt
Valuation: Avoiding the Winner's Curse

International Business

Peter Marber
Money Changes Everything: How Global Prosperity Is Reshaping Our Needs, Values, and Lifestyles

Fernando Robles, Françoise Simon, and Jerry Haar
Winning Strategies for the New Latin Markets

Investments

Zvi Bodie and Michael J. Clowes
Worry-Free Investing: A Safe Approach to Achieving Your Lifetime Goals

Harry Domash
Fire Your Stock Analyst! Analyzing Stocks on Your Own

D. Quinn Mills
Buy, Lie, and Sell High: How Investors Lost Out on Enron and the Internet Bubble

D. Quinn Mills
Wheel, Deal, and Steal: Deceptive Accounting, Deceitful CEOs, and Ineffective Reforms

John Nofsinger and Kenneth Kim
Infectious Greed: Restoring Confidence in America's Companies

John R. Nofsinger
Investment Blunders (of the Rich and Famous)…And What You Can Learn from Them

John R. Nofsinger
Investment Madness: How Psychology Affects Your Investing…And What to Do About It

Leadership

Jim Despain and Jane Bodman Converse
And Dignity for All: Unlocking Greatness through Values-Based Leadership

Marshall Goldsmith, Vijay Govindarajan, Beverly Kaye, and Albert A. Vicere
The Many Facets of Leadership

Marshall Goldsmith, Cathy Greenberg, Alastair Robertson, and Maya Hu-Chan
Global Leadership: The Next Generation

Management

Rob Austin and Lee Devin
Artful Making: What Managers Need to Know About How Artists Work

J. Stewart Black and Hal B. Gregersen
Leading Strategic Change: Breaking Through the Brain Barrier

William C. Byham, Audrey B. Smith, and Matthew J. Paese
Grow Your Own Leaders: How to Identify, Develop, and Retain Leadership Talent

David M. Carter and Darren Rovell
On the Ball: What You Can Learn About Business from Sports Leaders

Subir Chowdhury
: *Organization 21C: Someday All Organizations Will Lead this Way*

Ross Dawson
: *Living Networks: Leading Your Company, Customers, and Partners in the Hyper-connected Economy*

Charles J. Fombrun and Cees B.M. Van Riel
: *Fame and Fortune: How Successful Companies Build Winning Reputations*

Amir Hartman
: *Ruthless Execution: What Business Leaders Do When Their Companies Hit the Wall*

Harvey A. Hornstein
: *The Haves and the Have Nots: The Abuse of Power and Privilege in the Workplace… and How to Control It*

Kevin Kennedy and Mary Moore
: *Going the Distance: Why Some Companies Dominate and Others Fail*

Robin Miller
: *The Online Rules of Successful Companies: The Fool-Proof Guide to Building Profits*

Fergus O'Connell
: *The Competitive Advantage of Common Sense: Using the Power You Already Have*

W. Alan Randolph and Barry Z. Posner
: *Checkered Flag Projects: 10 Rules for Creating and Managing Projects that Win, Second Edition*

Stephen P. Robbins
: *Decide & Conquer: Make Winning Decisions to Take Control of Your Life*

Stephen P. Robbins
: *The Truth About Managing People…And Nothing but the Truth*

Ronald Snee and Roger Hoerl
: *Leading Six Sigma: A Step-by-Step Guide Based on Experience with GE and Other Six Sigma Companies*

Susan E. Squires, Cynthia J. Smith, Lorna McDougall, and William R. Yeack
Inside Arthur Andersen: Shifting Values, Unexpected Consequences

Jerry Weissman
Presenting to Win: The Art of Telling Your Story

Marketing

Michael Basch
CustomerCulture: How FedEx and Other Great Companies Put the Customer First Every Day

Jonathan Cagan and Craig M. Vogel
Creating Breakthrough Products: Innovation from Product Planning to Program Approval

Al Lieberman, with Patricia Esgate
The Entertainment Marketing Revolution: Bringing the Moguls, the Media, and the Magic to the World

Tom Osenton
Customer Share Marketing: How the World's Great Marketers Unlock Profits from Customer Loyalty

Bernd H. Schmitt, David L. Rogers, and Karen Vrotsos
There's No Business That's Not Show Business: Marketing in Today's Experience Culture

Yoram J. Wind and Vijay Mahajan, with Robert Gunther
Convergence Marketing: Strategies for Reaching the New Hybrid Consumer

Public Relations

Gerald R. Baron
Now Is Too Late: Survival in an Era of Instant News

Deirdre Breakenridge and Thomas J. DeLoughry
The New PR Toolkit: Strategies for Successful Media Relations

Contents

ACKNOWLEDGMENTS xix

FOREWORD xxi

PART I: MANAGING THROUGH TOUGH TIMES 1

CHAPTER 1   INTRODUCTION 3

HITTING THE WALL 5

FEWER WORRIES 6

CONVENTIONAL WISDOM 11

RUTHLESS EXECUTION 15

LEADERSHIP 15

GOVERNANCE 18

CRITICAL CAPABILITIES 21

PART II: LEADERSHIP: DEALING WITH RUDE
AWAKENINGS 25

CHAPTER 2   LEADERSHIP: STRATEGIC RECALIBRATION
AND THE BUSINESS PHILOSOPHY 27

THE RUTHLESS EXECUTION CHECKLIST 28

STRATEGIC RECALIBRATION 28

REVITALIZING THE CORE 29

READING THE ENVIRONMENT 33

PORTFOLIO MANAGEMENT DISCIPLINE 34

USING THE PERFORMANCE PORTFOLIO
FRAMEWORK 35

GUIDELINES FOR STRATEGIC RECALIBRATION 38

THE ART AND SCIENCE OF PORTFOLIO
MANAGEMENT 40

THE BUSINESS PHILOSOPHY 48

COMMUNICATING CONSISTENTLY 52

CHAPTER 3 THE COMPETITOR: JACK WELCH'S
BURNING PLATFORM 53

NUMBER 1, NUMBER 2 55

UNIQUE AND HIGH-SPIRITED 57

QUANTUM LEAP 58

FEET ON THE STREET 60

WORK OUT 62

SIX SIGMA 65

CHAPTER 4 THE RECALIBRATOR: JOHN CHAMBERS
MANEUVERS THE CISCO GROWTH ENGINE
THROUGH STORMY TIMES 71

MOST VALUABLE COMPANY 75

HEALTHY PARANOIA 77

PRIMED FOR GROWTH 78

THE CRESCENDO SUCCESS 80

A WEAKENED ECONOMY 86

SIGN OF RECOVERY 90

PART III: HOW TO PLAY THE GAME 93

CHAPTER 5   GOVERNANCE: TOUGH RULES FOR TOUGH
             TIMES 95

    THE RUTHLESS EXECUTION CHECKLIST 95
    ACCOUNTABILITY 96
    PERFORMANCE MANAGEMENT SYSTEM 100
    ALL MEASURES ARE NOT CREATED EQUAL 102
    DISCIPLINE 107
    THE DISCIPLINE OF CAPITAL INVESTMENT 108
    STRIVING FOR CONSISTENCY 110

CHAPTER 6   THE EXECUTIONER: LOU GERSTNER
             IMPOSES A NEW DISCIPLINE AT IBM 113

    LEADING COMPUTER COMPANY 115
    HEADING FOR TROUBLE 117
    KEEPING IBM TOGETHER 119
    FALLING ASLEEP ON THE JOB 121
    CONSTRUCTIVE IMPATIENCE 123
    NO OVER-PROMISING 125
    STRESSING THE SERVICES SIDE 126
    A DESK IS A DANGEROUS PLACE 127

CHAPTER 7   THE IMPORTANCE OF CONSISTENCY:
             HARRY KRAEMER ALIGNING THE NEW
             BAXTER 131

    DON'T FIXATE ON EXPECTATIONS 135
    STRATEGIC BYWORDS 138
    SHORT TERM AND LONG TERM 140

PART IV: BREAKING THROUGH THE WALL 143

CHAPTER 8   CRITICAL CAPABILITIES: ACTIONS THAT
MAKE A DIFFERENCE 145

THE RUTHLESS EXECUTION CHECKLIST 145

VIGILANT PRODUCTIVITY MANAGEMENT 147

COST MANAGEMENT 147

WORKING CAPITAL MANAGEMENT 149

TECHNOLOGY-DRIVEN PRODUCTIVITY
IMPROVEMENT 150

TALENT MANAGEMENT 152

BRINGING ON THE BEST 155

FOCUSED CORPORATE TRANSACTIONS 157

AN AGGRESSIVE ACQUIRER 160

CHAPTER 9   THE ACQUISITIVE MAN: THE STEVE
KAUFMAN CASE 165

NEW GROWTH STRATEGY 168

LARGEST DISTRIBUTOR 170

CHAPTER 10   THE MERGER MAN: DAN VASELLA
BRINGS NOVARTIS TO GREAT SUCCESS
177

BADLY BEATEN 180

U.S.-STYLE CAPITALISM 181

SPEEDING UP DEVELOPMENT 187

WINNING FDA APPROVAL 188

PHYSICIAN TURNED BUSINESSMAN 189

CHAPTER 11   MR. PRODUCTIVITY: LARRY BOSSIDY
USES INFORMATION TECHNOLOGY TO
MOLD A NEW HONEYWELL 193

    DRIVING OUT COSTS 198
    THE PUSH FOR SIX SIGMA AND DIGITIZATION 199

PART V: WHAT IT ALL MEANS 203

CHAPTER 12   FINAL THOUGHTS 205

    RUTHLESS EXECUTION INDEX 210

    INDEX   217

ACKNOWLEDGMENTS

Any business leader, consultant, or teacher worth the money would own up to the fact that we learn more from the people we work with, the clients we serve, and the students we teach, than they do from us. To admit anything else is sheer arrogance. In my almost 20 years working for and later advising some of the great corporations, I have had the privilege of rubbing shoulders with many business leaders who served to enrich my understanding of the business world. Just about every client, colleague, and student I have had the honor of working with has shed light on how business leaders look at their world and how they ultimately make decisions. Far too numerous to name individually, I want to thank all of these people for helping shape the ideas that eventually found their way into *Ruthless Execution.*

I want to particularly thank three people who I have had the honor of working with and who have personally influenced my thinking and approach to business problems and this book in a significant way: Larry Bossidy; my friend and former partner, John Sifonis; and my old boss, Pete Solvik. I have learned a tremendous amount from these men during my tenure with them, but above all, they taught me that "brutal focus" and "straight talk" are essential for success.

A number of executives took significant time away from their busy days to sit down with me to talk about their experiences. I thank them especially: Lew Platt; Larry Kittelberger and his ace Karen Suchenski; Stephen Kaufman; Harry Kraemer and his super team of George Rafeedie and Deborah Spak; and John Whybrow. I want to particularly acknowledge Lew Platt for honoring me with the Foreword to this book.

My experience with the editorial team was, simply put, the best I've ever had. Tim Moore and his team at Financial Times Prentice Hall proved to be the kind of editors who make life easier for an author. They had a way of gently prodding me to refine the text of this book into something that was as reader-friendly as possible. Thank you all for steering me through this long voyage. You are world class.

I want to express my gratitude to author Robert Slater for some crucial advice he gave in shaping the structure and writing of this book. We first met when I was with Cisco Systems, and he was writing his book on the company, *Eye of the Storm*. When I mentioned to Slater that I too was working on a book idea and would welcome some of his expertise, he agreed to stay in touch and weighed in with a number of insights, many of which found their way into the book. I thank you for being there on so many occasions.

Finally, I want to thank the two people who made the day-to-day enjoyable throughout the course of this book: my beautiful wife, Jennifer, and our incredible son, Nathaniel. Every book project cuts into precious family time, and this book was no exception—missed parties, weekends, vacations, late evenings spent working. It is a tremendous burden on family and friends and not something you can ever make up. Jennifer, I know not to apologize anymore. I am truly grateful to both of you for the gifts of encouragement and humor that you give me each day.

FOREWORD

When I joined Hewlett-Packard (HP) in 1966 as a process engineer in the Medical Products Group, I had little idea that one day I would have the chance to take over the leadership of the company. But 26 years later, I was asked to become the chief executive officer (CEO), and I served in that post for the next seven years, from 1992 to 1999. As the CEO of HP, we set ambitious goals and hoped that we could go from strength to strength. We wanted to grow a great company built on its founder's legacy, "The HP Way." But, I could not be certain that we would grow as much as I had wanted. After all, there were certainly going to be factors beyond my control that could stymie us.

I'm proud of the fact that when my period of leadership came to an end in 1999, HP was ready to move to its next phase of maturity. And, our financial results were personally quite satisfying. HP's revenues grew 187 percent to $47.1 billion during my tenure as CEO, while earnings grew 436 percent. Our share price went up to $114 a share, an eight-fold increase. Most gratifying to me, HP had broad respect as a business; it was one of America's most admired companies.

But this did not mean that all went smoothly every year. The economy was bound to turn sour one day. It was all but inevitable that some of our products that we had high hopes for would not sell so well. I've learned all too painfully that a business reversal can happen after a strong growth period; and it can happen with very little warning.

Figuring out how to make a quick, solid recovery from those bumps in the road became one of my greatest challenges. That is why I have been delighted to read *Ruthless Execution; What Business Leaders Do When Their Companies Hit the Wall* and to find that it offers a set of guidelines on how to bounce back from an unexpected business reversal. As the book notes, it is only when a company hits the wall that the business leader is truly tested. It's then that the leader has to decide whether to keep stoking the fires of growth or to pull back to fight another day.

It's then that the greatest pressure is on the CEO to take the company back to its days of glory.

I like the way *Ruthless Execution* talks about companies hitting the wall. There is a strand of optimism that runs through the book, conveying a sense of impermanence about business reversals. The book gives you new confidence that it is possible to recover from hitting that wall.

The focus of this book is on the common strategies that business leaders who have broken through these proverbial walls employ. If business leaders learn what those common strategies are and implement them in their businesses, they are probably going to enjoy a resurgence of success. That is what this book argues eloquently.

Just by way of example, one strategy that the book talks about is balancing between the short term and the long term. Business leaders who have dealt successfully with hitting a wall have learned how to handle that balancing act. Author Amir Hartman has a nice term for this strategy; he calls it STRATEGIC RECALIBRATION.

I've learned in my own business career that you have to grapple with that balancing act both in good times and in bad. Some would argue that it's easier to deal with this kind of balancing in good times. I'm sure that's not the case. In good times it's very easy to put the pedal to the metal and get all the growth you can. Things are going well; it's easy to grow; it is very easy during those times to overlook the moves that one has to make to guarantee a better long-term future for the company. I would argue there are times when the right strategy is probably to back off on current growth in order to have the company better positioned for the future.

The true value of this book is in giving executives an understanding of what it means to engage in ruthless execution, which taken together is a set of strategies that business leaders have found useful in recovering from hitting the proverbial wall. The message of the book is simply this: Hitting a wall need not be the end of the road for your company. It will be painful. You might even find yourself attacked in the media. Wall Street may lose confidence in your company for some time. But, as this book so wisely points out, business setbacks do not need to spell disaster. There is a way out. But it will take some figuring out.

LEW PLATT,
FORMER CHAIRMAN AND CEO,
HEWLETT-PACKARD COMPANY,
JULY 2003

MANAGING THROUGH TOUGH TIMES

1

INTRODUCTION

Ruthless execution is the method and strategies that business leaders employ to break through performance walls. My friend and former partner, John Sifonis, and I first employed this term in 1996 when we were doing work for Hewlett-Packard (HP). Subsequently, the phrase appeared prominently in our book *Net*

Ready (McGraw-Hill, 2000) as a way to sum up the actions key to getting a company "Internet-ready." During the research process for this book, and in searching for a way to "package" my findings, it became clear to me that the same term captured the essence of the strategies that business leaders execute to overcome tough times.

Few books exist on tough times and how to deal with them. Books on American corporate life have tended to proffer advice on how to steer a business to success and glory. For the past two or three decades, as the stock market drove skyward, as the economy went from strength to strength, as business theorists argued that growth was good, business leaders craved roadmaps that assured them of the same success that others were enjoying.

Authors of business books have focused on the strategies and the kinds of culture a business needs to do well. They have largely skipped over the topic of how to cope with business reversals. As long as the economy prospered, no one cared to write about—or read about—the morbid subject of business reversals.

That has all changed now.

With the advent of a turbulent economy, with the increasing realization that business resembles a roller coaster more than a rocket ship, with more and more companies plummeting from their peaks, a new, painful fact of life in business has become clear: COMPANIES NO LONGER CAN ASSUME A STEADILY UPWARD PATTERN OF GROWTH. Invariably, companies are going to get into trouble from time to time, enough trouble for the ups and downs to become a consistent pattern. Accordingly, books on business subjects must deal honestly and realistically with these reversals and offer some practical ways to overcome these setbacks. That is precisely what *Ruthless Execution: What Business Leaders Do When Their Companies Hit the Wall* does.

HITTING THE WALL

I define HITTING THE WALL as a rude awakening that occurs when a company has enjoyed consistent high-level performance, but comes up against some new factor: a downward turn in the economy, a lack of product innovation, growth that occurs too rapidly, a missed market opportunity, or as is most often the case, ineffective execution. Because of that new factor, the company can no longer sustain profitable growth for a significant period of time, at least two years. It is typically rude, because most business leaders don't see it coming, and it is often preceded by strong performance.

In case anyone doubted that reversals have become more and more a business norm, the fact is that 257 public companies, with a total of $258 billion in assets, declared bankruptcy in 2001, eclipsing the 2000 record of 176 companies with $95 billion in assets. By May 2002, another 67 companies had gone bust, among them *Fortune 500* enterprises for which failure had always seemed out of the question.

Hitting the wall—and it's an ugly thing to declare—has become a new reality for many companies. However, hitting the wall does not automatically mean failure to survive. During the bear market of 2001 and 2002, businesses suffered sharp reversals even while falling short of bankruptcy. Some 26 of the largest American firms saw at least two-thirds of their market value crumble, including blue-chip names such as HP, Cisco Systems, AOL Time Warner, The Gap, and Charles Schwab. This kind of near trouble is a recent phenomenon: No major firm suffered such a fate in the 1990 bear market.

In this book, there is no attempt to explain why companies hit the wall. That sort of analysis has been the subject of a number of other books and articles. More important to note is that what causes reversals is most often controllable. Irrespective of cause, almost always it is an inability to focus and execute that is at the heart of the problem.

Indeed, if hitting the wall has become a new business norm, if business reversals haunt the leadership of companies more now than at any other time, it makes sense to offer urgent guidance on how to return to the path of success, or how to recover after HITTING THE WALL.

For the past three years, I have been investigating companies in this predicament, companies that over the long run have been strong performers, but from time to time have fallen into periods of stagnation. From my research, I have come up with a way of looking at these companies that I have found extremely useful.

The focus of this book is on business reversals and the need to shepherd business leaders through those reversals because, quite frankly, corporations are passing through a new, more complex, more worrying age. The long and the short is that it's far more difficult to be a successful business leader today than ever before.

FEWER WORRIES

In earlier days, business leaders had fewer worries. Their jobs were simpler. They faced less pressure, requiring fewer, easier decisions. Because there was less pressure to succeed, there was concomitantly less dishonor and embarrassment over failing.

Certainly, major corporations had their ups and downs in the past; some even went through distressing bankruptcies and fatal collapses. Yet, that gentler period was witness to a more consistent flow of business. Businesses did not achieve, as some do today, hyper-growth rates of 30, or 40, or even 50 percent a year, but neither did they fall flat on their faces overnight, as has happened all too frequently in the past year or two as company after company has watched helplessly as huge inventories languished on shelves and massive debts mounted.

That gentler period allowed business leaders to survey the big picture, and then scurry for the golf courses and quiet dinners, less out of laziness than boredom.

The chief executive officers (CEOs) of the 1950s were free for those dinners because of an emphasis at the time on decentralized authority and command-and-control styles of management that allowed business leaders to delegate more decision-making to underlings. As a result of these hands-off types of management, businesses appeared to run themselves.

In days past, the status quo was king within the realm of business leadership. Conservative managers resisted any decisions that altered their companies' strategic focus on business fundamentals. The goal was to preserve core competencies, not to pursue high-risk initiatives that smacked of innovation and aimed at growth. There was little motivation to challenge the status quo and go beyond one's comfort zone.

As long as change within the business environment, when it came, was incremental, and did not require sudden, dramatic decisions from people at the top, that kind of don't-rock-the-boat mentality was fine. But the quickened pace of change in the last few decades—changes wrought by globalization of new technologies, by sharper competition, and by rapid production innovations—has created a business environment that is confusing, complex, and uncertain.

If the simplicity and certainty of a previous business era exalted the status quo, today's business environment, ever so chaotic and unpredictable, has put increasing pressure on business leaders to keep a competitive edge. To get ahead of the competition, companies have felt the need to pursue high-risk innovation in pursuit of company growth.

Business theorists like Peter Drucker have argued persuasively that what made companies great was growth! If companies did not grow at 8 or 9 percent a year, Drucker insisted, they were not really growing. Growth was not only good in his view, it was essential for survival.

Companies in the 1990s appeared to understand Drucker's analysis. Growth was in the air and it was fun breathing it, profitable too. Every few months, companies produced new computer-based products; stepped-up research created a flourishing biotech industry. Perhaps the greatest source of innovation and a spur to growth was the Internet.

The pressure on companies to grow has been very real, urged on not only by business gurus with our latest management tools, but also by other proponents as well. Venture capitalists opened their pockets eagerly; Wall Street dispensed initial public offerings (IPOs) like candy; analysts, both on the Street and in the media, judged companies by how much they grew in a year. Even as Lou Gerstner was leading IBM's resurgence, erasing billions of dollars of losses, the media scolded him for not attaining double-digit growth. The message was clear: If you're a growth king, the media sings your praises. As an example, *Fortune* magazine wondered whether John Chambers might not be the best CEO for achieving 70 percent annual growth rates over a five-year period at Cisco Systems.

If the 1980s was the "greed is good" decade, the 1990s produced a "GROWTH IS GOOD" mentality that made company growth at any cost seductive and difficult to avoid. Yet, the very pursuit of growth and innovation took companies into unchartered, dangerous waters. Growth brought companies to new financial highs, but it also all too often brought them to shattering new lows.

To survive in this go-go environment, reflected most visibly by the Internet business bubble that took hold in the late 1990s, executives were led to believe that playing the growth game vigorously would lead to unconditional success. They were in for a rude awakening and would pay a heavy price. John Whybrow, former executive vice president of Royal Philips Electronics, recalled just how seductive a time the Internet bubble was for executives: "Yes, we were seduced, both personally and professionally. It seemed like a continual stream of people was coming to my office to say you're wrong (to ignore the Internet), you're just an old-fashioned manager; the days of bricks and mortar are over. You should be building this or that company on the American West Coast for a billion-dollar investment." Whybrow's instincts proved correct as eventually the bubble burst.

As was evident with "the bubble," unconditional success all too often leads to rude awakenings.

A business reversal may come suddenly, as it did for John Chambers' Cisco Systems in the winter of 2000–2001; or gradually, as it did at General Electric (GE) in the late 1970s and early 1980s, and at IBM throughout the 1980s. During the early 1980s, few at GE other than the new CEO, Jack Welch, acknowledged that GE was heading for the shoals. Though many in a company prefer to deny its existence, the rude awakening shouldn't be hard to miss: First, sales are flat or start declining; soon leadership starts cutting so that operating margins don't take a hit; eventually Wall Street picks up on the theme; then comes a drop in the stock price; that dismay quickly infects employees and customers who may both display a lack of confidence in the company. Whether the rude awakening occurs abruptly or slowly, at some point, the company begins to drift.

Figuring out how to avoid a business setback is far more difficult than it might appear, as business leaders discovered in the early part of 2001 when product demand suddenly dried up across the

U.S. economy. Executives who had become preoccupied with the growth side of their businesses suddenly felt defenseless against the dramatic downturn in the economy; they were forced to react to the sudden loss of business in dramatic, often extreme terms, laying off thousands of people, taking charges on now-useless inventory, and canceling plans for future growth.

A way out exists that can keep business leaders from taking these extreme measures. They need not be the norm. It is possible to find instructive guidelines on how to recover from rude awakenings by doing nothing more than studying business leaders who have gotten themselves through these messes. THE LEADERS WHO HAVE PULLED THEMSELVES THROUGH THESE SETBACKS SHARE CERTAIN BEHAVIOR PATTERNS. Business leaders who wish to cope successfully with reversals can learn a lot from these behavior patterns that fall under the broad-ranging phrase "RUTHLESS EXECUTION."

In early 2000, watching companies struggle with the collapse of the "New Economy" and ensuing economic downturn, I became interested in uncovering the ingredients that leaders who overcame these struggles shared. That became the thrust of three years of research, which eventually made it clear that THE NOTION OF RUTHLESS EXECUTION COULD SERVE WELL AS A POWERFUL AND OVERARCHING FRAMEWORK FOR GUIDING BUSINESS LEADERS THROUGH THE REVERSALS THAT INEVITABLY AND FREQUENTLY OCCUR.

The research examined companies that had at one time or another suffered setbacks. The goal was to discover what practices these companies employed that helped them break through the wall. The means was to study a diverse set of industries and companies, large and small, using surveys, company documents, research reports, publicly available financial data (10-Ks), and where possible interviews with key business leaders. At times, I served as a consultant to these companies, enabling me to build case studies of these enterprises.

One key discovery gleaned from the research is that in times of uncertainty—and there is no more uncertain time than a business reversal—BUSINESS LEADERS WHO HAVE SUCCEEDED IN BREAKING THROUGH VARIOUS WALLS HAVE OUTPERFORMED THEIR PEER GROUPS WITH RESPECT TO RELATIVE MARKET SHARE GROWTH AND STOCK PRICE PERFORMANCE.

CONVENTIONAL WISDOM

Conventional wisdom has dictated that only two ways of exerting leadership in troubled or uncertain times exist:

■ THE RUN-AND-GUN STRATEGY—This way of thinking creates a vision and growth engine and seeks to drive that vision as fast as possible. As long as the economy remained in good shape, business leaders following this approach were treated like celebrities. But danger arose when the economy soured and these same business leaders failed to take care of the fundamentals of their businesses. In pursuit of hyper-growth, some business leaders lost sight of certain business imperatives, believing that as long as their companies were growing, it was simply not necessary to give any kind of priority to business fundamentals. There was no "rainy-day" strategy for these leaders, a strategy that would have allowed these leaders to put the brakes on growth-oriented initiatives long before an economic downturn could ruin those initiatives. Unfortunately, some growth-bound leaders appeared to lack the will and operational skills to activate the requisite fundamentals. "In growth mode," said Lew Platt, former CEO of HP, "being a great cheerleader, keeping the company culture together, and communicating well with Wall Street become important." One can probably get away during those times as a leader without having great operational skills. But that usually comes to haunt you later. Having the right kind of operational skills is fairly important because otherwise you are inadvertently making mistakes that will cost you when that downturn inevitably comes, and it always comes. "Every time you overbuilt in good times you wind up paying the price when bad times come," says Platt.

■ THE SLASH-AND-BURN STRATEGY—This strategy focuses on performance-oriented initiatives in times of peril. It applies more to companies that face great peril rather than simply tough times. This form of leadership calls for companies to take drastic actions, such as massive cost-cutting procedures, layoffs, etc., to keep the place from going under. It is therefore not very popular among business leaders who prefer to believe that they would never have to undertake such desperate actions.

This either/or approach to business leadership has been popular since it conforms nicely to the notion that most want to believe: A business leader faces either good times or bad times, nothing in between. In good times, one behaves in one way; in bad times, in another.

But, the run-and-gun/slash-and-burn framework is far too limited. It simply does not adequately account for most situations. Indeed, most business leaders feel strongly that the norm for them is facing periods in between these two extremes, thus making the run-and-gun/slash-and-burn framework virtually irrelevant. However, a third approach called *ruthless execution* is available, and it works far better for most business leaders. And, it provides business leaders with great opportunities to get past the rude awakenings.

It is possible, without too much difficulty, to characterize business leaders who rely on *ruthless execution* in some very specific ways, for they differ quite decisively from their colleagues.

Business leaders who pursue either of the run-and-gun/slash-and-burn approaches come with a certain impulsiveness and eagerness to opt for quick-fix solutions, particularly when faced with crises or a need to turn their companies around quickly.

Engaging in ruthless execution means that business leaders have the time and opportunity to study the issues, and then act on them. During tough times, leaders do not have to rush into making decisions, but just the opposite. They should take the time required and think prudently about what to do next and how to focus the company's efforts. Indeed, business leaders who have broken through walls have tended to be very fact-based and analytical in their approach to problem-solving.

Exhibiting patience is a definite requirement for making decisions in uncertain times, for the last thing you want to do is to suggest that it is easy to revitalize an organization. One McKinsey & Company study,[*] for example, pointed out that of 492 software companies defined as struggling, just 13 percent of them were able to break through their walls. The software business is notoriously filled with struggling businesses, so this is an extreme example perhaps; nonetheless, it should not be assumed that the remedy is a trivial matter.

We've recently experienced a period where is seems like dark days have fallen on the corporation. Scandal has hit one major enterprise after another as executives have allegedly embarked on systematic, earth-shaking exercises in criminal greed. First it was Enron; then Arthur Andersen; Global Crossing, Adelphia, Tyco, and WorldCom followed. Corporate fraud, however isolated the above cases were, has taken on the appearance of a broad, generalized disease sweeping across the entire business landscape.

---

[*].   M. Bluming et. al., *The McKinsey Quarterly*, vol. 3 (2002).

In setting out the concepts and themes of this book, it is best to leave to others the analyses and lessons that will inevitably arise from these scandals. It makes more sense to examine the themes of this book as if these scandals had not occurred, or were occurring in some other environment. You might wonder about making such a distinction: Is not corporate greed, manifested through these allegedly fraudulent acts, a result of the pressures on business leaders mentioned previously? The answer is: Yes, corporate greed is certainly such an illustration, but it is far too simplistic to argue that putting an end to corporate greed will make it easier for all corporations to break through the walls that they will hit from time to time. The current corporate fraud relates to certain companies, but by no means to all. The concepts and themes articulated in this book relate to all companies.

To be clear, this book is not about fixing companies in crisis. Crises such as fraud or bankruptcy often require a slash-and-burn approach and intense media management. This book is about getting stalled companies performing again. Companies are going to get into trouble for all sorts of reasons, scandal being just one of them. The plain truth is that most large corporations—over 90 percent of all public companies—suffer rude awakenings from time to time; indeed, setbacks happen to these large enterprises frequently. Large, established companies can become complacent; they may become too bureaucratic to innovate; innovative enterprises may favor hyper-growth at the expense of discipline and rigor.

When companies find themselves stagnating, it becomes time for their leaders to engage in ruthless execution.

What is meant by *ruthless execution*? It means the way leaders and their teams behave, or in other words, the strategies they must adopt to break through the wall.

RUTHLESS EXECUTION

The strategies of ruthless execution are framed in three distinct categories that are already part and parcel of every executive's daily life: LEADERSHIP, GOVERNANCE, and CRITICAL CAPABILITIES. Within each of these categories, a number of practices will be elaborated on throughout the book. There is no suggestion that engaging successfully in any one of these strategies automatically allows you to break through a wall. The idea is to point out the common ingredients (or practices) that business leaders who have figured out how to break through the wall share.

It is possible to say, however, that business leaders who have successfully broken through the wall follow a logical sequence that roughly follows the order of this book. In other words, the very first step that a business leader should take in seeking to escape from a business setback is to recalibrate his or her strategies. I define STRATEGIC RECALIBRATION as the act of validating the direction and focus a company is going to take. In doing so, the company should identify and focus on key battlefields and realign its resources so that it is more effectively balancing between performance-oriented and growth-oriented efforts.

Those who engage in strategic recalibration must rearrange their portfolios of business initiatives; they must assess how they are allocating resources to various initiatives; they must set a course for the direction that their companies should take. At this stage, these leaders operate within the LEADERSHIP framework as they decide what it is they must recalibrate.

LEADERSHIP

LEADERSHIP frames the specific actions that drive strategic formulations, and to a degree, the characteristics that business leaders need to overcome business reversals. The focus in the leadership category is on strategic formulation.

Key questions to answer are:

1. What is important to your company? How do you fundamentally create value?

2. Are you effectively balancing between performance-oriented initiatives and growth efforts?

3. Has a clear focus been defined and effectively communicated throughout the organization?"

4. Can you drive this focus through the organization for effective optimization of resources?

Within the LEADERSHIP category, the focus is on the following two strategies:

■ ENGAGING IN STRATEGIC RECALIBRATION—As noted above, strategic recalibration validates the direction a company is going to take. It is, in effect, the process by which business executives achieve a proper balance between performance and growth efforts.

The performance side of a business encompasses the short-term items that are fundamental to the business's existence, such as being efficient, stabilizing core revenue, and hitting quarterly numbers to meet Wall Street's expectations. The growth side encompasses the efforts that are most inclined to lead to new revenue streams, new markets, and new products. Growth implies an emphasis on the "new" aspects of a company.

Part of getting over a business reversal is knowing when to engage in performance-driven initiatives and when to turn to growth-driven ones. You have to know what the right mix is.

■ DEVISING A BUSINESS PHILOSOPHY—The second practice under leadership is DEVISING A SHARPLY DEFNED BUSINESS PHILOSOPHY THAT CAPTURES EMPLOYEES AND

KEEPS THE COMPANY ON THE RIGHT COURSE. It also helps executives keep a clear focus on what really matters. Most important, it emphasizes doing the right things as opposed to doing things right. Others like to call this notion "culture," but I find the phrase "business philosophy" to be more appropriate. A company can have a culture that moves from one generation to another, making culture less indicative of what a company looks like at a given moment. A business philosophy emanates from the top, it is highly individualistic, and it tends to be identified with the CEO of the company. A business philosophy is more likely to offer guidance on what a company is all about at any given moment more than a culture, which can be vague and uninspiring. The single best illustration of a business leader who devised a sharply defined business philosophy was GE's Jack Welch. He weaved every aspect of business into a single, coherent, tightly drawn philosophy. There was no GE culture as such; but there was Jack Welch's business philosophy. For strong evidence of how much the business philosophy belonged to Welch, not GE, take a careful look at the post-Welch GE under the new chairman and CEO, Jeff Immelt. He has dropped a number of the familiar Welchisms in favor of his brand of business philosophy.

Next, business leaders say, "Okay, now that we know what we want to do, we need to figure out how to do it. We need to frame the rules of the game for recalibrating our business." Toward that end, the leaders operate within the GOVERNANCE framework, with accountability, performance management, and discipline as the main strategic drivers for determining how to engage in the recalibration process.

GOVERNANCE

GOVERNANCE spells out the rules of the game; it deals with issues such as the way decisions get made and the discipline that leaders impose on their teams.

Key questions to answer are:

1. Do you have a disciplined process for allocating resources and spending capital?

2. Do you use the right performance measures, and are you measuring the right things?

3. Do you have a disciplined performance management process in place?

Under this concept of governance, we will talk about the following three practices that are crucial to the business leader who wants to get over a business reversal:

■ ACCOUNTABILITY—As part of the effort to move beyond business reversals, executives must establish a system of accountability. It is not enough to decide what tasks people must perform. Certain executives must be given responsibility for making sure that those tasks are performed efficiently, effectively, and in the precise way that the tasks were meant to be done.

Executives who understand the importance of accountability often rely on a set of strategies that falls under the heading of "alignment." It becomes crucial to make sure that senior management and a whole host of elements within the company—and outside of it—are on the same page. Alignment, essentially same-page thinking, represents all those efforts by which a business leader makes sure that the company is working in harmony. With such alignment, there is a much better prospect that a system of accountability will work successfully. Among the elements that require alignment with senior management are all of the stakeholders: employees, suppliers, shareholders, Wall Street, etc.

■ PERFORMANCE MANAGEMENT SYSTEM—*Performance management* translates business strategies and incentives into deliverable results by using financial, strategic, and operating business measurements that gauge how close a company comes to meetings its objectives.

There is a definite relationship between accountability and performance management. For a company to expect its metrics to have an impact, someone within the company must be accountable for measuring business initiatives and determining progress.

Business leaders who do the best jobs at measuring do not try to measure too much. Because they strive for simplicity, they seek to be meticulous in what and how they measure. Measuring too many things in the business can be obstructive; it can slow things down. Focusing too much on metrics can affect execution adversely.

Those who engage in performance management effectively prune to only the critical metrics. They look at cash flow and other such measurable statistics and they employ different metrics for different phases of the business.

Companies that have been successful at breaking through the wall have certain characteristics with respect to what they measure. It makes sense to look at those characteristics.

■ DISCIPLINE—A company that is disciplined has the ability to keep performing in a rigorous and consistent manner. Among the ingredients that business leaders who have broken through walls have in common is a relentless pursuit of discipline, without enmeshing others in a bureaucratic maze.

Executives have understood that discipline means communicating messages that are consistent, straightforward, and easy-to-understand. They have understood that discipline means creating business plans that have clear-cut goals with reasonable time frames; it means that any employee falling within such a business plan always knows what they are expected to do, and how long it is supposed to take.

Leaders accountable for these types of business plans cannot expect those plans to operate without supervision and constant watchfulness. The disciplined executive is the one who pays attention to the business every day. To do otherwise is to allow complacency to seep into the running of the business.

The case studies in this book examine a pair of executives, Lou Gerstner of IBM and Larry Bossidy of AlliedSignal and later Honeywell International, who placed great importance on running their companies in a disciplined way. Both men understood that their companies, having suffered business setbacks, did not require major overhauling, of neither products nor personnel. What they needed was proper management. They needed people at the top who understood what it meant to get things done. Both men quickly identified the problems at their companies as a lack of resolve in getting things done quickly, efficiently, and effectively. There was no magic formula to setting things right. Both men knew that it would take continued hard work. But above all else, it would require the introduction of discipline.

Finally, after implementing the necessary strategies, business leaders are ready for the actual recalibration process to occur. They must put in place a number of CRITICAL CAPABILITIES that are, in and of themselves, the very essence of recalibrating. These critical capabilities include productivity management, talent management, and focused corporate transactions (mergers, acquisitions, and divestitures). It is through these critical capabilities that business leaders recalibrate their businesses in search of undoing business reversals.

CRITICAL CAPABILITIES

CRITICAL CAPABILITIES are the specific actions that executives drive to break through the wall. Critical capabilities are very action-oriented. They are the critical skills and delivery capabilities with which business leaders need to be equipped.

The key questions to answer are:

1. Are costs and productivity improvements in the DNA of the organization?

2. How good are you at finding and getting rid of non-performers?

3. What business functions should you keep and which should you let go?

In this section, the focus is on the following three critical capabilities that business leaders have employed in successfully overcoming business reversals:

■ PRODUCTIVITY MANAGEMENT—Companies that have been able to overcome previous business setbacks have two critical capabilities in common: They stress 1) cost and working capital management, and 2) productivity improvement.

Before these companies were entitled to move on and undertake initiatives that focused on growth, they had to make sure they had done a good job at these two critical capabilities. It is fair to say that succeeding at cost management and productivity are prerequisites for healthy growth. Without paying close attention to these two things, companies cannot regain the confidence of Wall Street or other factors in the financial community. As such, companies have found a key path to revitalization involves a focus on cost management, working capital, and productivity that brings them operational improvements quarter after quarter.

■ TALENT MANAGEMENT—More and more, one hears from business executives that they view their main task to be THE HIRING OF THE BEST TALENT AVAILABLE. An equally important task of business leaders is getting rid of the deadwood, whether at the executive level or among the grassroots staff. So crucial has this management of talent become that it has also become an important strategy in the executive's arsenal.

Managing talent not only has to do with hiring the best possible people, but also with getting rid of those who are bringing the company down. Indeed, finding great talent is often easier for business leaders than dropping the deadwood. Most business leaders acknowledge that nothing is more difficult in their jobs than dismissing employees, and the very worst thing they have had to do is to fire someone with whom they have worked closely.

A business leader intent on overcoming past difficulties must know how, among other things, to assure that the right leaders and managers are in place to get results. Business leaders increasingly assert that their most important task is to make sure the right talent is in place; some even say the rest of the business takes care of itself. That task is called TALENT MANAGEMENT.

■ FOCUSED CORPORATE TRANSACTIONS—Finally, there is the topic of FOCUSED CORPORATE TRANSACTIONS (MERGERS AND ACQUISITIONS, AND DIVESTITURES) under the category of critical capabilities. The yen to acquire new businesses is part of a company's natural ambitions for growth. Acquisitions become a critical capability for companies looking for ways to get past their existing business reversals. Getting rid of unwanted assets can also be a critical capability.

Indeed, the critical capability of making acquisitions has changed the face of American business. With so much emphasis placed on growth, it is no wonder that corporation after corporation has sought to build business by purchasing other firms. To some analysts, acquiring other firms is an impure, or at least, artificial act, as if the parent company had sought the easy way out by making the purchase. Companies that make a habit of acquiring others are accused at times of simply trying to boost their revenues through these purchases. Critics of this tactic believe that "pure growth" is that which is conceived and implemented internally. What is clear, however, is that companies that are more consistently acquisitive and strategic in their divestitures outperform their peers.

Throughout this book, case studies will be used to illustrate a particular ruthless execution strategy. The introduction of each case study is framed around a moment of time when the subject company has suffered a reversal. These studies show how the company in question used one or more of the strategies to cope. You can benefit by employing one strategy or another in your own efforts to emerge successfully from a reversal.

Lastly, in Chapter 12, I introduce a Ruthless Execution Index. This index can serve as "sign posts" for business leaders who want to understand where they can improve their Ruthless Execution. I encourage you to revisit these practices on a regular basis.

It is now time to explore a pair of strategies that fall within the leadership category, strategies that executives have used successfully to break through the wall.

LEADERSHIP: DEALING WITH RUDE AWAKENINGS

LEADERSHIP: STRATEGIC RECALIBRATION AND THE BUSINESS PHILOSOPHY

"In good times it's very easy to put the pedal to the metal and get all the growth you can. . . . It's very easy to overlook the right moves that one has to make to guarantee a better long-term future for the company . . . There are times when the right strategy is probably to back off on current growth in order to have the company better positioned for the future."

Lew Platt,
Former Chairman and CEO,
Hewlett-Packard

THE RUTHLESS EXECUTION CHECKLIST

1. Are we better at what matters to our customers?
2. Are there key drivers that focus what we do and don't do?
3. Which strategic battlefields must we win?
4. Are we spending the right amount in the right areas to win these battlefields?

As noted in Chapter 1, leadership frames the specific actions that drive strategic formulations, and to a degree, the characteristics that key leaders need to overcome business reversals.

The term *leadership* is so common within the business framework that it almost seems unnecessary to define it. To make matters a bit more complicated, leadership can highlight many different things. However, I want to highlight specific aspects of leadership that are critical to breaking through a wall: strategic recalibration and the devising of a business philosophy.

STRATEGIC RECALIBRATION

Although executing the strategies presented in this book in sequence is not the only way to break through a wall, executives would do well to follow the order of this book. The first step they should take is to recalibrate their strategies. This means rearranging their portfolios of business initiatives, assessing how they are allocating resources for initiatives, and deciding what direction their companies should take.

Strategic recalibration, simply put, is the act of validating the direction a company is going to take and focusing on that direction. As companies attempt to validate that direction, they realign and reconfigure their resources so that they are balancing between performance-driven and growth-driven initiatives.

Many senior executives have virtually no experience in managing their companies through bad times. Unfortunately, when faced with performance walls, they slam on the brakes. They usually focus on across-the-board cuts, which they figure to be the fairest solution, but the results typically kill the good with the bad. They may indeed meet short-term goals, but they stymie the company's long-term growth capabilities.

Despite the real need for most business leaders to recalibrate their portfolios, very few companies have an established method for such an effort. A lack of process around such an effort can often exacerbate a company's poor performance. Because biases and politics tend to shape decisions and actions, they can often lead to an executive's mistaken belief that most products/services and customers are strategically critical when in reality few are.

The leaders I studied who were successful in breaking through performance walls had a keen understanding of their businesses and knew well what mattered to future performance and the details of how their companies created value. They made hard decisions based on operational excellence and growth as priorities. They placed top-line growth ahead of cost issues.

REVITALIZING THE CORE

Effective leaders understand that a company, after hitting the wall, must try to revitalize its core businesses and not wander off the path into diversified ventures that do not play to its core capabilities.

But how does one do those things? Companies must start by focusing on stabilizing and revitalizing their core revenues. The enticements to enter new markets are often out there and are hard to overcome. As markets expand, every company wants to get a large share of those markets. And, some companies that are doing well in one market conclude that they understand the principles of business well enough to migrate into other markets without asking whether they have that right. This is especially true of companies that have a strong cash position.

Good leaders know that a wise course of action is to take a good, hard look at their best customers. After all, these were the people who made their businesses a success at one point; they can do it again. These customers may want different products, or product upgrades; they may want better prices. Whatever they want, they were at one time the leaders' best customers. A key act of recalibration would be to get back to them as quickly as possible and make them a focus of the business once again.

These same successful leaders also appreciate that it need not be a handicap to engage in strategic recalibration during bad times. Some of the best business minds have used dismal economic periods to get a jump on their competition. Cisco Systems' John Chambers has used economic downturns to gain market share, to invest in possible breakaway strategies, and to look for new markets. Michael Dell exploited the 1990–1991 downturn to perfect his company's telephone ordering and demand-pull production system. Andy Grove, then-CEO of Intel, stepped up investments in cutting-edge plants and equipment, and launched the now-famous "Intel Inside" brand-developing campaign.

PORTFOLIO. WHAT PORTFOLIO?

Every business has a portfolio of initiatives that make up their "spend." The problem is most leaders don't realize they have a portfolio, and worse, they don't do a good job of managing the portfolio.

Many companies think in terms of portfolios of businesses. This makes sense in good times, when one can devise long-term strategies and be reasonably assured they will endure. But, managing through tough times and revitalizing an organizaion fundamentally takes focus. This is the goal of portfolio management. See Figure 2–1.

A key step for business executives in recalibrating their strategies is to rearrange their portfolios of business initiatives, the set of projects, investments, and other efforts that their businesses are working on and allocating resources and attention against.

Recalibrating by adopting a portfolio-of-initiatives strategy encourages executives to be more flexible, immediate, and action-oriented. The very notion of strategic recalibration is to monitor circumstances, to engage in rigorous analysis of each initiative, and to adapt to changing circumstances. There is

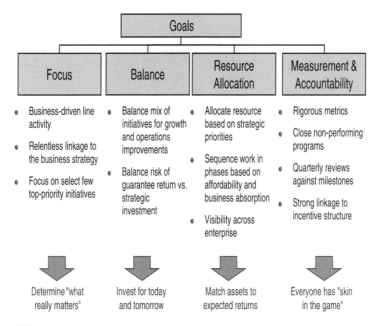

FIGURE 2–1
The goals of recalibration.

ample opportunity to alter initiatives in mid-course, which is a great plus. Among the critical qualities I found in the leaders I studied was an analytical, fact-based bent. The executives tended also to be unemotional about the act of strategic recalibration.

It should be clear by now that setting a new strategic focus—which is what strategic recalibration is all about—requires strong analytical capabilities. It requires a careful, but swift, examination of strategic options in a rigorous and thorough manner. It also requires discovering what truly matters in the marketplace.

For business leaders who are experiencing poor performance, there is nothing more important than to analyze precisely what creates value for their companies. The process of strategic recalibration is intended to deepen, indeed to sharpen that analysis, to make the whole process of scrutinizing the causes for that poor performance much more clear, much more visible. It is the unfortunate truth that many companies do not embrace the kind of rigorous analytical process that is needed at such critical times, preferring to make decisions in an ad-hoc fashion that keeps them from making true progress.

As part of that rigorous analysis, executives must constantly supervise the initiatives that could help them break through walls. They must treat each initiative as if it were a separate business, having the time and patience to uncover which initiatives are worth retaining and nurturing, and which need to be killed.

Engaging in that same meticulous probing, executives must make sure that new initiatives fall within core parts of their businesses. This means pursuing operational excellence; in short, making certain they have the fundamentals of their businesses down. They must also make sure that they do not neglect the growth side of their businesses, even in tough, challenging times.

Business leaders who pay attention to both the performance and the growth parts of their businesses simultaneously are truly engaged in strategic recalibration.

READING THE ENVIRONMENT

Reading the environment correctly is crucial when engaging in strategic recalibration. Business analysts note the rational, cool-headed approach taken by Lou Gerstner when he took over at IBM in the early 1990s. He argued that the environment was not going to change radically in the next few years and all his company had to do was execute properly, that is, with focus, and engage in strategic recalibration.

Unfortunately, the time allotted for a business leader to break through the wall is far shorter in the 21st Century than it was even a decade earlier because of the heightened media attention and increased watchfulness of Wall Street analysts. Because of this, I believe that Gerstner would not be given the same opportunity and timeframe today that he was given at an earlier date to fix his company outside the public glare.

As an example, we can look at how much time Carly Fiorina was "given" to make significant impact and fix HP when she became CEO in late 1999. The media and Wall Street paid far more attention to Fiorina than to Gerstner at the start of his CEO tenure. This could be for many reasons: among them the groundbreaking fact that she was a woman, that the world was in the throes of the Internet boom and it was thought that HP had fallen behind, that HP had just spun off Agilent Techologies and was already somewhat under the microscope, etc. Whatever the reason, the landscape had changed and she wasn't going to have the luxury of time in which to engage in strategic recalibration.

Portfolio Management Discipline

The performance portfolio framework that will be set out on these pages is a valuable frame of reference for illustrating strategic recalibration. It can help business leaders understand the focus or lack of focus of their organizations. I first introduced this framework with clients in the mid-1990s and subsequently in the book *Net Ready* as a way to assess IT investments. However, this framework is a valid mechanism to view any capital or resource-intensive investment, for example, a new plant, product, or acquisition.

The purpose of the framework is to enable a fact-based rationalization or prioritization of investments and resources that are getting allocated across a company. The framework suggests, for example, that a company might need to find more balance between performance and growth activities in order to earn the right to grow. As another example, the framework might suggest that a company is not engaging in enough performance-driven initiatives, or that the company is not disciplined enough, etc. Additionally, the framework can let a company know that it is doing enough on the performance side, but not enough with growth-based initiatives.

The framework, therefore, is a useful device to help establish priorities, because, quite frankly, today's executives confront a multitude of opportunities, a plethora of decisions that overburden them. Rather than set priorities, most simply take on too many unfocused activities.

It becomes vital to know when and under what circumstances to engage in strategic recalibration and move between performance and growth-driven initiatives.

USING THE PERFORMANCE PORTFOLIO FRAMEWORK

How do you use the performance portfolio framework? I often employ this framework with clients in mapping exercises that help them understand the investments and projects currently underway and whether they are aligned with the strategic battle-fields they must win. In addition, it helps leaders determine which business initiatives they should undertake and what their risk profiles should be. The mapping takes place around core drivers that shape the value of a company. The core drivers become the parameters within the portfolio framework for the mapping exercise. The framework allows a move away from the traditional performance growth paradigm, unlocking various options in the selection of business initiatives.

Business criticality and newness/innovation are the two key variables, which make up the axes of the framework and which drive the value of a company. These dimensions, selected from certain empirical evidence, are critical in predicting a company's value.

Driver number one, newness/innovation, goes on the horizontal axis. Essentially, this defines what new value you will bring to the marketplace and, therefore, how much new value it will bring to your company. The question to be answered is: How new or innovative is a particular initiative? As you move along the horizontal axis from left to right, the left-hand side of the chart is not so new, while the right-hand side is extremely new. Moving from right to left, the more de facto or standard an initiative becomes, the less new or innovative it is.

Driver number two, business criticality, goes on the vertical axis, with business initiatives in the bottom half representing less "business-critical" initiatives than those in the upper half. Business criticality essentially defines how critical an initiative is to your business strategies. It measures the degree to which a particular business initiative directly drives core differentiating factors for a company. The more business-critical something is, the more strategic it is to a company; thus, it is more of a risk to a company if it's not executed effectively.

Mapping business initiatives along the two dimensions of innovation/newness and business criticality allows you to understand the impact of high-ranking initiatives on your organization.

Figure 2–2 is the performance portfolio framework. You can use the framework to map the location of any business initiative, and thus gain a better understanding of why you are doing a certain business activity at a certain time and stage.

The portfolio framework is organized into four quadrants along the two dimensions of business criticality and innovation/newness:

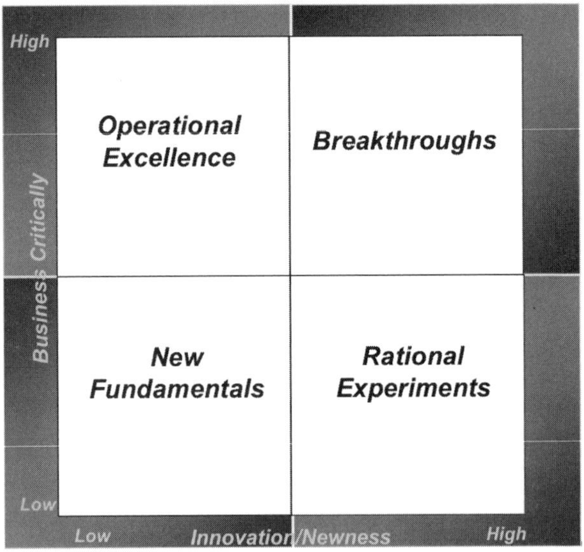

FIGURE 2–2
The performance portfolio framework.

■ NEW FUNDAMENTALS—The most basic, low-risk, non-critical operations of a business are placed in the bottom left-hand side of the framework. New fundamental initiatives are productivity-driven and aim at cutting costs; they are not strategic or core differentiators to the company.

They typically do not directly impact shareholder value. Not excelling at new fundamentals efforts might place a company at risk, but doing them very well will not guarantee success. Understanding which of the new fundamentals are really important and which you should stop doing is essential. The average company has too many investments in this area that are not essential.

■ OPERATIONAL EXCELLENCE—Initiatives in this quadrant are high in business criticality, medium in risk, and focus on transforming mission-critical initiatives, as well as stabilizing and improving core revenue. Projects and investments in this area are fundamental for competitive differentiation. They are more strategic than innovative, and very essential to delivering value. The objective is to execute these efforts as efficiently and with as little friction as possible. For manufacturers an example of this type of initiative is managing an organization's supply chain. Companies with limited investment or poor execution in operational excellence are at significant risk.

■ RATIONAL EXPERIMENTATION—Initiatives that fall within this quadrant experiment with new business models and new go-to-market strategies, and are low to medium in risk. The best advice with such initiatives is: If they work, keep them; if they don't—and most don't—shift your resources quickly.

By trying to create new markets and revenue growth in non-mission-critical areas, these initiatives tend to be new or innovative to the market, and if they fail, the business still survives. Not yet core to a business, they aim typically at new value creation as opposed to driving efficiency; they tend to focus on new organizational practices surrounding new products or services that might become strategic. The focus is on seeding new growth and new revenue streams. The key word is RATIONAL; choosing a select few that are focused is good. Fishing for growth is not.

■ BREAKTHROUGH STRATEGIES—This upper right-hand quadrant is the path-breaking, high-risk arena of business initiatives that involves transforming a core strategy or basic business approach. It can also involve transforming the nature of an entire market.

High in business criticality, plus high in innovation, these business initiatives, when successful, can rupture an industry, altering the competitive balance among companies. While relatively new, these initiatives quickly become strategic.

These groundbreaking initiatives tend to be oriented toward new business models, new revenue streams, and innovative, go-to-market strategies that have a very significant impact on the market itself. They are, by their nature, rare and fleeting (quickly turning into industry standards). What investments are you seeding for such opportunities?

Seeding a select number of such opportunities is critical for future performance.

GUIDELINES FOR STRATEGIC RECALIBRATION

Here, I would like to introduce a quick-start guide for engaging in strategic recalibration, to give you a brief description of how to go through each step in the process of strategically recalibrating:

■ STEP 1: DATA COLLECTION—This is the fact-gathering
stage, when you take inventory of all the business initiatives
that the company is currently executing, plus all the initiatives that are under consideration for the near future. (See
Figure 2–3.). Unfortunately, my data tells me that most leaders face dilution to their initiative portfolios due to inconsis-
tencies in investment selection. This inevitably leads to
under-funding, duplicative efforts, conflicting goals, and the
allocation of resources to non-strategic efforts. To effectively

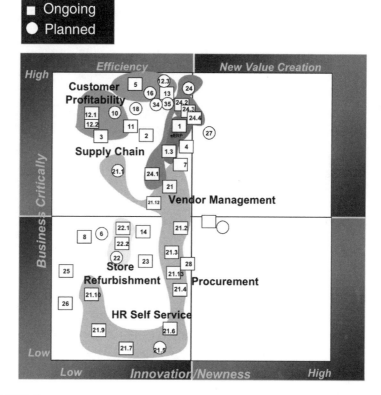

FIGURE 2–3
Each business unit and functional area should map its set of planned and existing programs (groups of
projects and investments that together drive value). In this example, the numbers represent individual
project components and the shaded areas represent larger programs.

recalibrate their portfolios, leaders must a) create a process by which effective investment comparisons can occur across the company, b) build a mechanism where objective and fact-based prioritization is the norm, and c) enable a rhythm for the reallocation of resources based on shifting priorities.

■ STEP 2: BUSINESS EVALUATION—In this step, you take a good, hard objective look at your customers and products and make some reasoned calculations of exactly how much each one contributes to the business, how profitable each one is, and how important each is to the overall operation of the business.

■ STEP 3: ACTUAL STRATEGIC RECALIBRATION—Among the questions you will answer at this stage are: a) What projects should you continue to do? b) What projects should you stop immediately? c) What corrective actions do you want to take to break through the wall? and d) What business initiatives are worth pursuing to aid those corrective actions?

THE ART AND SCIENCE OF PORTFOLIO MANAGEMENT

In studying successful leaders, it became apparent that there are key rules that are critical practices for effective portfolio management:

■ RULE 1—To drive business success, executives must MOVE AWAY FROM THE AD-HOC ALLOCATION OF RESOURCES AND TOWARD A STRATEGY OF ACTIVELY DEVELOPING INITIATIVES IN EACH OF THE FOUR QUADRANTS OF THE PORTFOLIO FRAMEWORK.

BACKGROUND: I've found that most companies, especially larger ones, have hundreds of projects underway, most of which do not drive value and are not aligned with the overall strategy. Without a clear-cut, highly defined strategy and key battlefields, the business leader finds that vast amounts of resources and precious blocks of time are easily wasted. By employing the portfolio framework, a business executive can make intelligent decisions that provide for a more reasoned, strategic, and efficient allocation of time, energy, and resources.

■ RULE 2—It is critical that business leaders build discipline into the portfolio management process.

BACKGROUND: As indicated earlier, most companies do not have an established process for managing the initiatives that fall across the company. Leaders who ruthlessly execute have in place a process by which they can:

1. Intelligently compare initiatives across a set of strategic imperatives.

2. Prioritize initiatives across the organization on an informed basis.

3. Effectively allocate resources to drive successful execution.

4. Better understand the ongoing costs and progress of the efforts.

5. Gain better visibility into the value (financial and strategic impact) that investments deliver for the company.

■ RULE 3—BUSINESS LEADERS MUST EARN THE RIGHT TO MOVE FROM A LOWER TO A HIGHER STATE OF BOTH BUSINESS CRITICALITY AND INNOVATION/NEWNESS. There is a right of passage that allows one to migrate from quadrant to quadrant.

BACKGROUND: Earning the right to make this passage requires superior performance in operational excellence and new fundamentals. Too many right-hand-side initiatives and investments without superior performance at the core is a recipe for trouble.

■ RULE 4—BUSINESS LEADERS NEED TO FOCUS ON A SELECT SET OF CRITICAL INITIATIVES. THE STRATEGY OF LETTING A THOUSAND FOWERS BLOOM SIMPLY DOES NOT WORK. Leaders who ruthlessly execute focus on a few critical initiatives that improve the core business and seed growth.

BACKGROUND: Although business leaders need to build a portfolio of initiatives with activity in each quadrant, they WILL IMPROVE LONG-TERM PERFORMANCE ONLY BY SUCCEEDING IN THE ACTIVITIES IN THE UPPER QUADRANTS. The temptation to seed numerous growth opportunities is always strong, but successful leaders place their efforts on a select few (2 or 3 at most). The urge to over seed is especially powerful for companies whose cash flows and cash position are strong because they feel they have the funds to experiment.

STOP THE MADNESS

To reduce cost inefficiencies and to focus on strategic projects, one retail company implemented a company-wide process and tool to assess the expected revenue contribution of its projects and identify promising growth areas as well as areas of consolidation. This effort resulted in a 60 percent reduction in the number of active projects, while improving the financial and strategic impact.

■ RULE 5—DO NOT EXPECT THE SAME RETURN ON INVESTMENT (ROI) OR RISK EQUATION FROM EACH BUSINESS INITIATIVE. All business initiatives are not equal. Each quadrant has distinct risk characteristics that form the basis for the type of project portfolio a business executive builds.

Accepting tradeoffs spreads the risk and creates optimum opportunities for saving money and creating new value.

BACKGROUND: Employing a financial portfolio as a metaphor for the portfolio of business initiatives is appropriate because most people are intimately familiar with the notion of financial portfolios.

The four quadrants of the portfolio framework can be thought of as being analogous to investing in bonds (new fundamentals), blue-chip stocks (operational excellence), an IPO market or venture financing (rational experimentation), and emerging markets (breakthrough strategies).

Your tolerance for risk and what the competition is doing shape the kind of portfolio that is best for your company.

To delve further into the metaphor:

- NEW FUNDAMENTALS = bonds; low risk. While you won't beat a market quickly, it's the smart, safe way to proceed.

- OPERATIONAL EXCELLENCE = blue-chip stocks; higher risk. These offer nice, steady returns. They are important in good and bad times.

- RATIONAL EXPERIMENTATION = IPO market or venture financing; even higher risk. Many efforts fizzle out; occasionally, you hit pay dirt.

- BREAKTHROUGH STRATEGIES = emerging markets; highest degree of risk. These strategies also offer the highest rewards.

This financial metaphor helps you realize that not all business initiatives are equal. In the same way that you would not expect the same returns from bonds as from high-tech stocks, you would not expect the same returns from new fundamentals investments as those from breakthrough strategies.

Executives who treat all investments alike do so to their detriment. By measuring initiatives in the same way, they inevitably fund them alike, which is a huge error! Business initiatives need to be treated differently; their efficacy should be measured differently, funded differently, and organized differently.

Figure 2–4 is the performance portfolio framework when viewed from the frame of reference of the financial metaphor.

■ RULE 6—BUSINESSES THAT ARE UNDER-PERFORMING VERSUS THEIR PEERS MUST FOCUS MORE OF THEIR ATTENTION ON NEW FUNDAMENTALS AND OPERATIONAL EXCELLENCE INITIATIVES.

BACKGROUND: Executives can get easily lured into a "let it ride" mentality that quickly brings them over to the rational experimentation and breakthrough strategies quadrants.

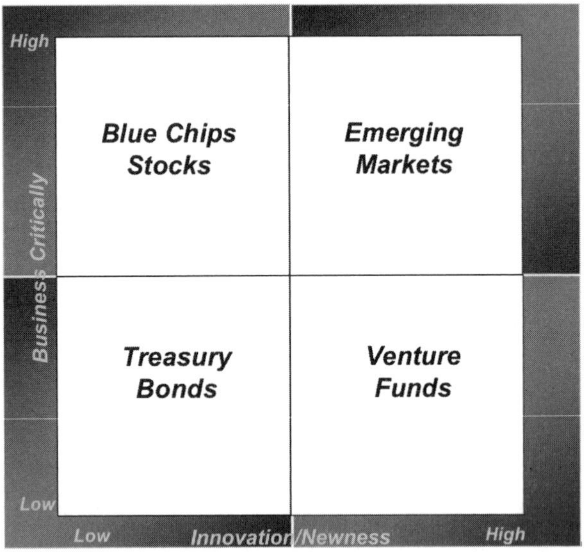

FIGURE 2–4
The performance portfolio framework and financial metaphor combined.

Such executives would be better off focusing on left-hand-side initiatives. This is easier said than done. I have yet to know of an executive who is not tempted by, if not lured toward, high growth and quick profits.

Yet that misplaced focus—lurching to the right—leads executives to hold unhealthy business portfolios, incurring the wrath of the financial markets. Viewing a company's core business in decline, characterized by a swift drop in earnings, the markets do not look positively at growth-oriented investments and soon the company gets into financial trouble. Forced to tighten capital spending, it begins its cutbacks by killing off the very same tempting quick-growth initiatives.

Companies must learn to allocate their "spend"—their capital investments (and resources)—differently. Keep in mind that "best of breed" firms tend to allocate the vast majority of their "spend" on left-hand-side initiatives in the new fundamentals and operational excellence quadrants. Some 60 percent of their "spend" tends to be allocated within operational excellence, and another 30 percent on new fundamentals, and 10 percent goes to right-hand-side initiatives.

Is There a Doctor in the House?

In contrast to these leading companies, most companies have unhealthy portfolios. My research indicates that over 40 percent of companies allocate 80 percent of their capital investment and resources to new fundamentals initiatives.

Most successful business leaders tend to recalibrate by focusing on operational excellence. However, cost-cutting alone is not enough; seeding future growth is an imperative as well. Still, right-hand side-growth programs will fail without a strong operational base. Critical weaknesses in the core business must be addressed before a company can start allocating significant spending on growth efforts.

The goal of strategic recalibration, that is, of building and managing a portfolio, is to manage the short-term operational improvements of a business and seed growth. But most companies do not achieve such a balance, leaving them with unhealthy portfolios. Most companies allocate attention to too many activities at once.

These companies are at significant risk. Not only do financial markets punish them as their earnings decline, but the same markets scorn their growth initiatives, reflecting the failure of the companies to earn the right to grow.

Other companies err by devoting most of their attention to growth and new value creation activities (rational experiments and breakthrough strategies). This was certainly true for most of the dot-coms and many traditional companies.

What does a balanced portfolio look like? Or, to put it somewhat differently, what is the ideal outcome of strategic recalibration? Achieving a good balance does not at all mean having the same number of initiatives in each quadrant. The poor success rate of rational experiments, and the rarity and fleetingness of breakthrough strategies, usually means that companies need a greater number of rational experiments than one would think. THE KEY IS TO FOCUS ON A FEW AND THEN PROVIDE THE NEEDED FUNDING AND RESOURCES TO FOSTER SUCCESS.

Too often, businesses fall into "portfolio traps" which do not allow them to effectively engage in strategic recalibration. Among such traps are:

- HESITATION—For most companies that find themselves in tough environments, where business trends are emerging but not necessarily posing an immediate threat, it is natural to just wait and see. Added to this, there is often a lack of fact-based insight which makes visibility to these trends problematic.

■ STICKING WITH THE FAMILIAR—This portfolio trap is characterized by the new fundamentals quadrant, where a company allocates over 80 percent of its attention to these efforts. This trap is often hard to get out of even when there are compelling arguments and environmental signals to make changes.

■ HALF-HEARTEDNESS—Some companies place many small bets on new initiatives, but end up very cautious. Without clear-cut revenue or profit prospects, it becomes difficult to justify large investments. Under pressure to bring in positive quarterly results, companies have trouble making long-term commitments. While leaders face difficult tradeoffs between creating short- and long-term value, spreading investment resources across too many efforts ultimately dilutes the productivity of the portfolio.

■ PIONEERING—These companies are able to create radical new products and transform an industry. While it is tempting to be a bold innovator, business leaders I studied avoided the "pioneering trap" by returning to basics, earning them the right to grow. Focusing excessively on breakthrough strategies—though it worked for Microsoft and Apple—probably means a company is not a leader.

A significant part of strategic recalibration is knowing when to seek growth. Not all growth is good. Executives should not simply look for a new product or new market, but rather they should MAKE SURE THAT THE KIND OF GROWTH THAT IS PURSUED CREATES VALUE FOR THE COMPANY.

THE BUSINESS PHILOSOPHY

What is meant by a business philosophy? It is a set of guidelines or directives that helps leaders communicate and institutionalize what's important to their businesses. Business leaders establish these guidelines, which form a basic ingredient of a company's culture, to help colleagues run their businesses. Business philosophies are useful for executives who are struggling with what steps to take to break through walls. Business leaders who have successfully overcome reversals rely on business philosophies that embrace all the ingredients of *ruthless execution.*

Business philosophies emanate from the top, they are highly individualistic, and they tend to be identified with the head of a company.

It is frequently said that great companies require great cultures. But the features that comprise company cultures are often vague and fuzzy, and are far too general to provide employees with operational roadmaps. In fact, organizational culture can often be an inhibiting factor for change and renewal. It can breed inertia and a sense of complacency. Whereas what is needed to manage though tough times is focus, action, and doing things differently. On the other hand, a *business philosophy*, if tightly scripted and highly delineated, offers clear guidance to employees.

The driving element of the IBM culture has been "THINK"; but, think about what? How should one think? A driving element of other cultures is to put the customer first. But how do you do that specifically? Some cultures call for listening to customers. But which customers do you listen to?

In contrast with all this, a business philosophy is specific and deals with practical, everyday issues. GE's Jack Welch espoused his "Number 1, Number 2" strategy as part of his business philosophy, and everyone understood without any doubt what he meant: A company must strive to become number 1 or 2 in its markets or else get out of that business. When Welch said that companies should become "boundaryless," he admitted that he had just made up the word and it was awkward, but everyone knew precisely what he wanted to convey—and GE employees began knocking down boundaries that had impeded communications and the smooth flow of business.

Because cultural elements tend to be unspecific, it is that much more difficult for executives to get past business reversals by adhering to those elements. But by listening to a leader articulate a business philosophy, executives have a far more focused and delineated roadmap for how to behave.

Executives who take the time to put together a coherent, tightly scripted business philosophy are going to be able to energize and motivate their employees at a time when they are typically less motivated, during a period of struggle and stagnation. The benefits of putting together a business philosophy should be self-evident. A business philosophy provides meaning to the strategies and goals of a company, making them easier to understand and therefore easier to implement. The business philosophy provides clear "signposts" to employees, explaining to them how things should truly be; and, of critical importance, it helps create a sense of energy that will help to achieve the strategies and goals. The crucial benefit of the business philosophy is to help everyone place the emphasis on doing the right things rather than doing things right. Emphasizing doing the right things is another way of talking about strategic recalibration: It is figuring out where the company should be focusing, as opposed to doing a lot of things that effectively fall outside that focus.

The absence of a business philosophy is a prescription for chaos, lack of focus, and inefficiency. An effective business philosophy helps get employees to understand what is important to the company and what is not.

The best business philosophies contain certain "universal" elements: Business leaders make sure that everyone strives to get jobs done—to ruthlessly execute. They set priorities and take actions based on those priorities.

Once a business philosophy is created, executives display a set of traits that reflects how they manage in-line with that business philosophy. These leaders of the *ruthless execution* school are decisive, but impersonal, no-nonsense and cerebral, and very demanding. In short, they know how to drive discipline within their companies.

They display a healthy, introspective attitude toward their companies. They evaluate the health of their companies objectively, assessing where their companies' strengths and weaknesses lie. They try to avoid falling into the trap of simply blaming external factors for their companies' setbacks. They are very fact-based.

Perhaps the greatest value of *ruthless execution* is helping business leaders determine whether their companies are simply in difficult times or in crisis. Mostly, these leaders find that their companies have fallen within a period of uncertainty, and they search for business philosophies appropriate for such times. Realizing that, they can understand that it makes little sense to take drastic action (across-the-board layoffs, for example), or to change long-range strategic visions. Rather, they require a business philosophy that is sensible, demanding, and disciplined.

Such a cool-headed, detached approach permits these leaders to deal more selectively with various ways to break through walls. Engaging in *ruthless execution*, in short, means not acting suddenly or randomly; it means not simply taking across-the-board actions; it means taking into account the differences that exist within a company.

THE SIX-MONTH SHUFFE

When leaders don't know what is really driving their poor performance, they invoke the "two quarter rule" for recovery. It is an innocuous statement to the analyst community that things will improve in six months, thus buying them some time to figure things out and enough time for the analysts to forget the rule was invoved in the first place.

Those leaders who have really understood the value of creating a business philosophy have communicated it relentlessly, with targeted messages to all constituents (employees, management team, shareholders, etc.). Most important, they have seemed to live by very clear rules when it came to communicating with their constituents:

- STRAIGHT TALK—The rule here is to have only clear and honest discussions on what the company needs to get done and what is expected of people. The rule insists that everyone face and understand the reality of the situation.

- NO SURPRISES—Here, the rule is to be consistent, to make sure everyone is on the same page. It means being very clear about the focus and key battlefields that the business needs to take on. It means setting very clear expectations, being up-front with everyone. It means being clear about what needs to be done and not concealing important issues, but putting them front and center.

- JUST THE FACTS—This rule argues against getting emotional about assessing the situation and communicating actions. The discussion here should include evidence, including numbers, about why you want to go in one direction as opposed to another. There should be facts behind the message.

■ KEEP PROMISES—It's not enough to talk straight, to be consistent, and to give the facts. You've got to deliver. You've got to do what you say you are going to do. If you don't, nothing else you say (or do) will matter.

COMMUNICATING CONSISTENTLY

Being able to communicate regularly and consistently to stakeholders is at the heart of any business philosophy. A business leader who says one thing one day and another the next confuses employees, and produces a negative effect on shareholders and Wall Street, two institutions that no one wants to embitter. With a purpose of uniting the company behind a clear-cut goal, the business philosophy has less of the feel of a vision, and more the sense of a rallying cry for short-term action.

In articulating a business philosophy, a business leader acts more like a cheerleader than a business executive. Being a cheerleader does not automatically mean a business leader is charismatic or charming, though at times a John Chambers comes along. Most business leaders are just ho-hum speakers, but some of the best leaders are the ones who know how to weave a business philosophy in a way that gets communicated effectively to large bodies of people.

The next chapter will provide the first case study, a look at a business leader who, better than most others, has utilized a business philosophy as a key ingredient to break through the wall. That leader is GE's Jack Welch.

THE COMPETITOR: JACK WELCH'S BURNING PLATFORM

B ack in the early 1980s, in his first few weeks in office as chairman and CEO of GE, Jack Welch understood what few around him did, that the company was in serious trouble, and that serious changes were needed. His diagnosis was not popular, even less so were his solutions.

Welch, of course, has been dissected and analyzed in a hundred different ways by business thinkers who have tried to explain his overwhelming success. In this chapter, the singular focus is on how Welch dealt with the fact that his company, in the early 1980s, was about to face a rude awakening.

Remember the main argument of this book: LEADERS WHO HAVE PULLED THEMSELVES THROUGH VARIOUS SETBACKS CLEARLY DEMONSTRATE CERTAIN COMMON PRACTICES. EMPLOYING THESE PRACTICES IS THE SAME AS ENGAGING IN RUTHLESS EXECUTION.

Building and institutionalizing a business philosophy is critical in getting a company performing again. No business leader has employed the strategies of devising a business philosophy as adroitly as former GE chairman and CEO Jack Welch. To get the company on his side, to energize the company for the tasks ahead, he created a BURNING PLATFORM, wrapping it up in a single neat phrase: HE WANTED GE TO BECOME "THE MOST COMPETITIVE COMPANY ON EARTH." This was the catchphrase around which everyone in the company congregated. Welch used the phrase often in speeches and interviews, whenever he wanted to encapsulate what he was trying to do at GE. It had the virtue of being succinct and serving as a rallying cry.

In addition to his burning platform, Welch laid out a tightly focused BUSINESS PHILOSOPHY that essentially answered almost every question about how to conduct business. By adhering to that philosophy, call it the "Jack Welch Way of Doing Business," GE employees could implement the burning platform. It was a business philosophy that clearly emanated from the top, totally from the mouth of the CEO. Above all else, Welch's business philosophy offered a roadmap, or set of guidelines, to employees on how to make decisions.

Since the platform had to do with making GE more competitive than anyone else, Welch decided to focus on a number of critical areas: 1) GE and the marketplace: its businesses had to be the best in their markets; 2) efficiencies: GE's personnel and infrastructure had to be the most cost-efficient possible; and 3) the talent pool: GE had to acquire and promote the best of the best.

GE's business philosophy helped shape its transformation. Throughout much of the 1990s, it was the most successful company on the planet and Jack Welch was constantly touted as the consummate business leader of the era.

When he took over GE in 1981, the company had annual sales of $25 billion and earnings of $1.5 billion, with a $12-billion market value, tenth best among U.S. public companies. In 2000, the year before Welch retired, GE had $129.9 billion in revenues and $12.7 billion in earnings. In 2001, GE's revenues grew to $125.9 billion and earnings rose to $14.1 billion (Welch stepped down in September 2001).

From 1993 until the summer of 1998, GE was America's market cap leader. GE stock averaged a return of 24 percent a year during Welch's first 18 years. The stock climbed 40–50 percent each of the years from 1995–1999. Its market cap soared to over $400 billion during Welch's final years as CEO. *Fortune* magazine selected GE as "America's Greatest Wealth Creator" from 1998–2000.

NUMBER 1, NUMBER 2

When he became the CEO of GE in April 1981, Welch had the good sense and vision to understand what no one else could see: His company was about to hit a wall. Foreign competitors, especially in Asia, were springing up, offering cheaper products based on cheaper labor. GE was under-performing. Only a handful of GE's 350 business units had become number 1 or number 2 in their markets: lighting, power systems, and motors. The only GE businesses that were coming in with good results on a global basis were plastics, gas turbines, and aircraft engines. And only GE's gas turbines unit led its market overseas.

Welch saw that manufacturing in the United States had become less profitable, and yet, in 1970, 80 percent of GE's earnings were derived from its traditional electrical and electronic manufacturing businesses. GE businesses such as plastics, medical systems, and financial services were doing okay, but they provided only one-third of the entire 1981 corporate earnings. A few other GE businesses, such as aircraft engines, spent more than they earned.

When Welch sought to invoke his burning platform—when he argued that GE had to become more competitive—he was considered an alarmist. No one wanted to endorse his seemingly radical re-engineering ideas. Welch, however, knew all too well how dependent GE had become on the manufacturing side of the business, and how costly that dependency would become if things were not rectified.

In developing a business philosophy that would help GE break through its wall, Jack Welch displayed a series of leadership traits that often exemplify the concept of ruthless execution. Certainly he was decisive; he had a no-nonsense attitude about him. He could be very demanding. Most important, he knew how to impose discipline on his organization. Not all of the traits that are congruent with the ruthless execution business philosophy are found in Welch, however. He is not impersonal or cerebral, for example. With regard to one of these traits—fervently believing in the power of facts—Welch had exhibited a certain ambivalence. Often he disparaged anyone who focused only on "the numbers." However, toward the latter part of his career when he instituted the six sigma program at GE, he grew fond of measuring and admitted that there was great value in paying attention to numbers.

UNIQUE AND HIGH-SPIRITED

On the day that he took over as GE's chairman and CEO, Welch told the board of directors and shareowners that he would like GE to be thought of 10 years down the road as a unique, high-spirited, entrepreneurial company, known for its excellence. His goal was to make GE the most profitable, highly diversified company.

Note what he did not say: He did not say he wanted GE to be the biggest (i.e., as measured in terms of revenues); nor did he even dream of the company acquiring the largest market capitalization in the country. HE WANTED GE TO BE THE BEST.

Allowing himself to think only in the short term, Jack Welch was bent on preserving GE's bottom line. He had plenty of great ideas, as he would acknowledge in later years, but he knew that it was far too early to try such ideas out.

One of his ideas—an important part of the business philosophy that he devised—grew out of his early years as GE's CEO, when he was restructuring the company, downsizing people, and rationalizing factory operations.

DEVISING A BUSINESS PHILOSOPHY

In pursuit of growth, Welch wanted only those businesses that were number 1 or 2 in their markets in the GE portfolio.

As a result of this restructuring, the business could employ more aggressive tactics, such as in pricing, and have the resources to develop new products.

Without the Number 1, Number 2 strategy, Welch said, inflation would start to impede worldwide growth. There would be no room for a mediocre supplier of products and services. Successful companies in such a slow-growth environment would be those that searched out and participated in growth industries and insisted on being number 1 or number 2 in every business they were in. They would need to be the number 1 or number 2 leanest, lowest cost, worldwide producers of quality goods and services, or they would have to have a definite technological edge in some market.

He downsized the GE payroll, ending the "no layoff" policy that had characterized the company and many other large U.S. firms. He sold $12-billion worth of businesses and purchased $26-billion worth of others. And, he pared GE's workforce from 412,000 to a mere 229,000.

To Welch, keeping people in place who contributed little or nothing to the company represented a failed strategy. It was a major reason why a company under-performed. GE's key competition in the early 1980s was coming from overseas enterprises that paid their employees less and achieved higher productivity rates. To compete successfully with such companies, GE had to upgrade equipment and cut employee rolls.

Another significant part of Welch's business philosophy was his frontal assault on the company's bureaucracy, DELAYERING (in his famous phrase) GE's management tiers. When Welch took over, each GE business had 9–11 organizational layers; a decade later, that figure had been cut to 4–6.

QUANTUM LEAP

It was also part of Welch's business philosophy to stick to fundamentals. He put value on taking incremental steps. He had little faith in pursuing growth for growth's sake. At times during his first few years as CEO, he imagined what it would be like to take one big swing and increase the size of the company by 30, or 40, or even 50 percent; but, he felt it would be irresponsible to make a systematic strategy based on what he termed the "QUANTUM LEAP," acquiring other major businesses.

Four years after he took over, Welch was ready to shift gears; he was prepared to tackle one king-sized growth initiative, stealthily pursuing the acquisition of the Radio Corporation of America (RCA). He termed this sudden, secretive approach to acquisition his "quantum leap."

Like GE, RCA was one of America's most important corporations. It set up the National Broadcasting Company (NBC) in 1926, entered the record industry in 1930, and was the first company to market a television set. RCA had interests in satellites, consumer electronics, and defense electrics. The deal was announced December 12, 1985, when GE and RCA agreed that GE would purchase RCA for $6.28 billion, or $66.50 a share. At the time, this was the largest non-oil merger ever. Prior to the deal, GE ranked ninth among America's largest industrial firms, and RCA was second among the country's service firms. When joined, they created a new corporate powerhouse with $40 billion in sales, making it the seventh largest company in the United States. Welch "grew" GE enormously with that one, swift, clever move.

The RCA gambit proved the exception rather than the rule in the mid-1980s. Welch would not take another "big swing," as he liked to call it, until just before his retirement in the year 2000, when he, seemingly without warning, decided that GE should purchase Honeywell.

On October 22, 2000, Welch stunned the business world by announcing that GE would buy the Morristown, NJ-based enterprise that made aerospace systems, power and transportation products, specialty chemicals, home-security systems, and building controls.

As a result of the Honeywell acquisition, GE would become far larger, in revenues, profits, and head count. The acquisition would add $24 billion to GE's annual revenues of $112 billion. GE's profits, at nearly $11 billion a year, would grow by another $2.5 billion, thanks to Honeywell. And, GE was getting another 120,000 employees, giving the new GE a combined head count of 460,000. (The planned merger fell apart when European regulators created conditions that Welch could not abide.)

FEET ON THE STREET

However, building a business philosophy was not enough. Welch had to COMMUNICATE HIS IDEAS and make sure that employees were listening to and adopting those ideas. He did not believe in videotaped presentations to thousands of employees. He preferred in-person visits to GE installations across the United States and around the world. He spoke constantly before GE audiences. To make sure that he was spending enough time getting his message across, Welch refused most media interviews, rarely appeared on television, and never joined the boards of other companies. The most important means by which he communicated his business philosophy was in his annual letter to shareholders.

Welch spent a few weeks during the early part of each year preparing his letter to shareholders that appeared in the *GE Annual Report*. In the early years of his chairmanship, Welch's letters to shareholders were fairly straightforward—he discussed how the company had done the year before and little else. But in time, Welch spent part of each letter describing one or more aspects of his business philosophy. By the late 1980s, most of each letter dwelt on his philosophy. Welch himself considered that letter one of the most important events of his year.

His process was systematic and nearly identical year after year. Alone and seated at his desk in his office at company headquarters in Fairfield, CT, Welch would dictate his first draft into a dictating machine. A secretary then transcribed the recording. All throughout the editing and rewriting of the transcribed draft, Welch still showed it to no one. Eventually, when he was ready, he showed it to 10 senior GE executives. After integrating their comments, he then produced a final version.

It was through these letters that GE personnel read, for the first time, about concepts such as "Number 1, Number 2," "boundarylessness," "speed, simplicity, and self-confidence," and "unleashing the brains and energy of employees."

Unleashing the brains and energy of GE employees became one of Welch's most serious challenges in the late 1980s and early 1990s. It stemmed from his desire to get the maximum productivity from his employee force. It took Welch some time before he realized that all the downsizing and restructuring that he had put GE through had taken a toll on the employees who remained. They were unsettled and in need of some nurturing from above. Relieved to survive the cuts, they still believed that they faced perilous futures as they confronted new plants, new bosses, and new jobs. Were their jobs truly safe now? They doubted it—not with Jack Welch in charge.

Welch concluded in the late 1980s that his employees needed to be empowered, and not because he felt sympathy for their unsettled feelings. He understood that he had to provide new motivation to employees to work harder. The secret was giving workers a feeling that they were "owners" of the business, not simply forgotten cogs in a faceless machine.

WORK OUT

In the fall of 1988, Welch came up with the solution: a company-wide program he initiated and called "Work Out." It was an effort that aimed at capturing whatever good ideas employees had for improving the company's operations and implementing those ideas. Over the next few years, every GE employee attended a Work Out session, where he or she was encouraged to propose ways to improve GE's operations. The head of the business unit where a Work Out session was occurring was required to appear in front of the group and decide on the spot to implement a select set of proposals. The program worked wonders. It got GE employees involved in the company's problems and challenges, and it forced everyone to look at the company's operations from top to bottom on a continuing basis.

Another anchor of Welch's business philosophy was to AVOID FOCUSING TOO MUCH ON ACCOMPLISHMENTS. To be sure, he encouraged colleagues to celebrate the attaining of financial goals—usually by going out and buying pizza for everyone (he did not believe in wasting money, either!). But on the whole, Welch had little love for milestones because he had little love for the past. He constantly put down the past as irrelevant to what he was doing—at that moment! He could not change it. He was, of course, proud of what GE had achieved during his time at the helm, but he preferred discussing the present and the future. He believed firmly there was nothing he could do to change the past, so the most he would do was to thank everyone for having a great year and then get on to talking about the future.

His strategy of "stretch," another anchor of the Welch philosophy, was clearly designed to make the company more competitive. This strategy aimed at getting the best out of his employees. Always willing and eager to reinvent himself and his company, always trying to convert change into an opportunity, always on the prowl for what should be the next corporate-wide initiative at GE, Welch simply did not sit still. He did not allow complacency. He wanted managers to "stretch" their financial goals and try to beat their budget objectives.

The first aspect of the stretch philosophy was to figure out performance targets that were achievable, reasonable, and within the company's capabilities. The key second aspect involved setting those sights higher—far higher—toward goals that seemed beyond reach, requiring superhuman effort to achieve.

Welch began his stretch program in the early 1990s. To have done it sooner would have asked too much of employees still reeling in the aftermath of the restructuring phase.

Creating what Jack Welch called a "LEARNING CULTURE" became an important part of his business philosophy in the 1990s. Welch liked to say that the operative assumption was that someone, somewhere, had a better idea. By sharing knowledge, GE businesses would gain a competitive edge, and that advantage would translate into higher earnings for the company.

He credited GE's learning culture with adding to the company's performance in several important ways:

■ Operating margins, under 10 percent for the last 100 years, had risen to 17.3 percent in 1999. In the first half of 2000, GE crossed the 18 percent threshold (the second quarter was over 20 percent).

■ Inventory turns, a key measure of utilizing assets, had run in the three to four range for a century, but was over eight in 1999.

■ Company earnings, which had shown only single-digit increases through the 1980s, had attained double-digit increases since 1992.

No matter how well GE did—and by the 1990s, the company had emerged as the nation's strongest—the CEO did not rest. In 1995, he took a big new step.

SIX SIGMA

WELCH SOUGHT TO MAKE GE "THE MOST COMPETITIVE COMPANY ON EARTH" by launching a company-wide initiative to improve the quality of GE's products and processes.

It had taken Welch a while, but now he was convinced that GE could no longer assert that its quality was high. Nothing was as fundamental to a company's performance as its quality and productivity. At first, this new push seemed a strange choice for Welch. GE had certainly made a dramatic point about having quality products and processes in the past. With respect to quality, the company's reputation was solid. Why was Welch so convinced that GE had to focus on quality as if its very survival depended on it?

One part of the answer: GE's products and processes had not yet attained world-class quality. Others like Motorola, Toyota, and HP enjoyed great reputations, but GE did not. Another part of the answer had to do with an error that Jack Welch later admitted to: He had long assumed that by instilling in his employees favorite Welch business values such as "the need to develop self-confidence" and to "look at business as a simple exercise" would in turn guarantee high quality for GE's products and processes. He assumed that improving the speed with which GE employees operated, improving their productivity, and raising their level of involvement in company decision-making would inevitably result in employees producing high-quality work. But it did not work. Certainly, under Welch's tutelage, employees became more self-confident and they came to appreciate the value of regarding business as simple. But, the level of quality failed to rise sufficiently.

Prior to the mid-1990s, Welch had been urging greater and greater levels of productivity from GE personnel. Yet, by the mid-1990s, employees insisted that greater productivity was only possible if there were improvements in the quality of GE's products and processes. These employees told Welch that too much time was being spent on fixing and reworking a product before it left the factory. This bottleneck cut down on GE's speed and reduced productivity. As a result, the performance side suffered.

SIX SIGMA

To improve things, Welch instituted the "SIX SIGMA" quality program. Six sigma is a measurement that enables a company to know how effective it is in getting rid of defects and variations from its business processes, products, and services. Literally, six sigma is reached when only 3.1 parts per million are defective.

In June 1995, Larry Bossidy, then head of AlliedSignal, spoke to GE's senior managers. Bossidy had been a vice chairman at GE, but he left in July 1991 to become the CEO at AlliedSignal. In 1994, Bossidy had launched a six sigma quality program at AlliedSignal. He told GE's business leaders that GE was a great company (he knew; he had worked there for 34 years), but that there was much to do for it to become greater. Welch had tremendous respect for Bossidy and decided that if six sigma was good enough for Bossidy, it was good enough for him. Welch launched the GE six sigma initiative in January 1996 at the company's annual gathering of its 500 most senior employees in Boca Raton, FL.

Many of Welch's strategies certainly paid off. By the year 2000, GE had achieved dominance or near-dominance in dozens of markets across the globe. It was number 1 in the world in industrial motors (manufacturers of electric motors), medical systems (imaging and diagnostic equipment), plastics (plastics for various sectors), financial services (credit and credit card leasing), transport (locomotives and rail equipment), power generation (turbines for power stations), information services (company networks, electronic commerce, etc.), aircraft engines (aircraft jet and other engines), and electric distribution equipment (control systems for industry). NBC, which includes general-interest programming and CNBC (business news), was ranked the number 1 U.S. network. GE was number 2 in the world in lighting (makers of light bulbs and neon strips) and household appliances (stoves, refrigerators, washing machines, etc.).

GLOBALIZATION was an important part of Welch's philosophy. He was ahead of his time; few U.S. businesses were going "global" when he pushed his own company-wide initiative. Almost from the time he became chairman and CEO of GE, Welch was convinced that GE's competitors were increasingly non-American, and that important opportunities existed for the company to grow by taking GE's business overseas.

In the early 1980s, globalization was largely an alien concept to many businesspeople. At that time, fully 80 percent of GE's revenues were derived from doing business in the United States. Most business leaders believed it was too complicated to operate overseas; Welch, on the other hand, saw globalization as a reality and as a great growth opportunity for GE.

In 1980, only two of GE's strategic businesses—GE Plastics and GE Aircraft Engines—were global enterprises. By 1999, international revenues had reached $45.7 billion, some 41 percent of GE's total revenues. In the fall of 2000, GE had 340,000 employees worldwide, with 140,000 of them working abroad.

Another aspect of the business that Welch nurtured for the sake of becoming more competitive was SERVICES. Welch understood that the great growth engine at GE was going to be his services business. This was a new concept. In 1980, the year before Welch took over, GE was almost totally a manufacturing company, with 85 percent of revenues deriving from manufacturing and just 15 percent from services. For decades, GE's growth had been inextricably bound to the company's manufacturing side.

The shift away from manufacturing and toward services started in the 1980s and gained great momentum in the 1990s. Though at first, the services side of GE was seen simply as a way of getting GE some extra business, in time, GE executives understood that a focus on services would enlarge the potential markets of GE businesses many times over.

In 1995, when Welch turned the services initiative to full throttle, GE had an $8-billion-per-year services business. In the next five years, by 2000, GE had grown the business to $17 billion. Even in 1990, GE was deriving only 45 percent of its revenues from its services businesses. Just five years later, in 1995, GE's manufacturing business constituted a smaller percentage of the total; it had gone from 53 percent to just over 40 percent.

The most important engine of GE's services growth—indeed the key engine of growth for all of GE—was GE Capital Services (GECS). In 1999, revenues for GECS reached $35.7 billion, almost half of GE's total revenue of $111.6 billion.

DON'T LEAVE HOME WITHOUT IT

Gradually, Welch's business philosophy emerged and was reflected in a laminated statement of values card that each GE employee was expected to carry at all times.

Following these values, Welch was implying, would help GE employees build "THE MOST COMPETITIVE COMPANY ON EARTH." Here are those values, first an early version, then a later one:

- Create a clear, simple, reality-based, customer-focused vision and be able to communicate it straightforwardly to all constituencies.

- Understand accountability and commitment and be decisive . . . set and meet aggressive targets . . . always with unyielding integrity.

- Have a passion for excellence . . . hate bureaucracy and all the nonsense that comes with it.

- Have the self-confidence to empower others and behave in a boundaryless fashion . . . believe in and be committed to Work Out as a means of empowerment . . . be open to ideas from anywhere.

- Have, or have the capacity to develop, global brains and global sensitivity and be comfortable building diverse global teams.

- Stimulate and relish change . . . do not be frightened or paralyzed by it. See change as opportunity, not just a threat.

- Have enormous energy and the ability to energize and invigorate others. Understand speed as a competitive advantage and see the total organizational benefits that can be derived from a focus on speed.

The above set of values has gone through slight changes lately. The latest version:

GE leaders . . . always with unyielding integrity . . . :

- Are passionately focused on driving customer success.

- Live six sigma quality . . . ensure that the customer is always its first beneficiary . . . and use it to accelerate growth.

- Insist on excellence and be intolerant of bureaucracy.

- Act in a boundaryless fashion . . . always search for and apply the best ideas regardless of their source.

- Prize global intellectual capital and the people that provide it . . . build diverse teams to maximize it.

- See change for the growth opportunities it brings . . . for example, "e-Business."

- Create a clear, simple, customer-centered vision . . . and continually renew and refresh its execution.

- Create an environment of "stretch," excitement, informality, and trust . . . reward improvements . . . and celebrate results.

- Demonstrate . . . always with infectious enthusiasm for the customer . . . the "4-E's" of GE leadership: the personal Energy to welcome and deal with the speed of change . . . the ability to create an atmosphere that Energizes others . . . the Edge to make difficult decisions . . . and the ability to consistently Execute.

Few business leaders have had such a clear-cut and tightly knit business philosophy as Jack Welch. Few leaders have thought about business with such care and devotion. By developing a Welch-like business philosophy and a burning platform, executives stand a better chance of moving beyond business setbacks.

The same benefits can come from engaging in strategic recalibration. To get a better understanding of how one CEO used this strategy to break through the wall, it is time to turn to Cisco Systems' John Chambers.

4

THE RECALIBRATOR: JOHN CHAMBERS MANEUVERS THE CISCO GROWTH ENGINE THROUGH STORMY TIMES

Business leaders who have figured out how to overcome business reversals have relied on two main strategies within the leadership category. The previous chapter on Jack Welch dealt with one of those strategies, the BUSINESS PHILOSOPHY. This chapter deals with the second strategy, STRATEGIC RECALIBRATION. Earlier, we defined strategic recalibration as the act of validating the direction a company is going to take. We said that in doing so, companies routinely realign their resources so that they effectively balance between performance-oriented and growth-oriented efforts. We noted that strategic recalibration was, in effect, the reconfiguring or recalibrating of the direction that a company would take.

One of the more interesting examples of how a business leader strategically recalibrated after his company had hit the wall is John Chambers, CEO of Cisco Systems.

KNOWING WHEN TO ENGAGE IN PERFORMANCE-DRIVEN INITIATIVES AND WHEN TO TURN TO GROWTH-DRIVEN ONES WAS PIVOTAL FOR JOHN CHAMBERS. By producing such high rates of growth in the early years of his leadership, Chambers established Cisco Systems as one of the most exciting companies of the era. But, that emphasis on growth left the company totally unprepared when the U.S. and world economies went into a tailspin in the winter of 2000–2001. Cisco, still a relatively young company, is now going through a maturation phase that requires it to focus more on performance-oriented initiatives. BECAUSE THERE WAS TOO MUCH GROWTH TOO FAST AND NOT ENOUGH PERFORMANCE DURING CHAMBERS' EARLY YEARS, CISCO SYSTEMS EVENTUALLY HIT THE WALL EARLY IN 2001.

Chambers' task at that point was to break through the wall. He knew that to break through the wall effectively, he would have to undertake a strategic recalibration by focusing on the performance side, by getting back to the basics, by imposing sharper discipline on the business, and by shedding, or more often squeezing and folding in, under-performing acquisitions.

By no means has it been an easy task for Chambers to break through the wall. This was a company that had mostly lived through the good times: It was relatively young (19 years old in the summer of 2003), born in a bull market and it had previously known mostly a bull market until the winter of 2000. Able to sustain high margins and remarkable hyper-growth reaching as much as 70 percent a year, it was unlike any company in the world in experiencing these kinds of numbers.

To go from that kind of company to one that is less giddy and more stable, one that relies less on external forces such as a continuing bull market for its success and more on its own operational skills, is a kind of maturation process that is linked directly with what I call strategic recalibration. None of this happens by snapping one's fingers. Such a maturation process takes time, especially for a young company that never had to be disciplined.

John Chambers, as a CEO, quite understandably got caught up in the enthusiasm for more and more growth. He "inherited" an enterprise that was in full growth mode. And as long as the business environment allowed for such growth, he did fine.

His company, Cisco Systems, developed the greatest growth engine of the "New Economy." As such, he appeared to be the perfect model for us, the prime example of a CEO who figured out how to marginalize the performance side of business, and give great focus to the growth side. For as long as Chambers succeeded—and did he ever succeed!—he provided a superb illustration of how to "grow" a business.

Until as recently as early 2001, Chambers was touted as the king of the Internet, its chief promoter, the "go-to" person for anyone—prime ministers, finance ministers, CEOs, chief information officers (CIOs)—who wanted to know where the Internet was heading. Displaying leadership characteristics routinely associated with growth-oriented CEOs, Chambers became the visionary for the Internet and for high tech in general. His speeches were full of predictions and projections, and were laced with examples of what the future would look like: It would be a place where telephone voice service would be free, where data and voice would merge into one "converged" telephone/computer technology, and where the Internet would become the single most important business tool of the era.

He was adept at COMMUNICATING HIS MESSAGE, a talent essential for a growth-oriented CEO. When he began his career, he actually suffered a case of stage fright; but, in subsequent years, he got over that dread and became one of the most forceful speakers in corporate America.

It was Chambers, more than anyone else, who glamorized the Internet and insisted that business leaders could not survive without a heavy investment in this new and fascinating business tool. So clear-minded and impressive was Chambers that political and business leaders alike flocked to hear his pearls of wisdom.

Among those pearls: Chambers and his team explained how they had improved productivity and efficiency by putting numerous business functions on the Internet. And, those pearls were backed up impressively by the spectacular performance of his company.

By the spring of 2000, Chambers' Cisco Systems had risen to the pinnacle of the high-tech world. It was the premium model of a company that "got" the Internet. Its products, routers, and other networking gear provided the infrastructure for the Internet. Internally, Cisco's processes and functions exploited the Internet better than any other U.S. firm. By manufacturing a full spectrum of products, excelling internally at utilizing the Internet and intranet for measurable productivity gains and cost savings, and actually making a profit, Cisco Systems seemed the ideal meld between the Old and New Economies.

MOST VALUABLE COMPANY

On March 27,2000, Cisco Systems became the nation's "Most Valuable Company" with $531 billion in market capitalization. Cisco remained at the top of the heap only for that one day, but it was a spectacular achievement.

A year earlier, Cisco Systems had the tenth highest market cap. When Chambers took over as president and CEO in 1995, the company's market cap had been only $9 billion. That led *Fortune* magazine to give Chambers one giant pat on the back, suggesting that his leadership at Cisco from 1995–2000 had to have been the greatest years any CEO had ever enjoyed. Cisco had reached a $100-billion market value in 1998—only eight and one-half years after going public—making it the fastest company to reach that mark in history. The previous record holder had been Microsoft, where Bill Gates took almost 11 years to achieve the milestone.

Among the beneficiaries of Cisco's skyrocketing stock were Cisco employees, several thousand of whom became millionaires by virtue of the stock climbing 8,000 percent in the decade since it went public early in 1990 at $18 a share. In 1999 alone, Cisco's stock rose 162 percent, trading at $72 a share. It would climb to a high of over $80 a share in the spring of 2000. At that point, it was still considered the blue-chip stock of the New Economy.

The stock reflected Cisco's spectacular revenue growth: In 1995, Chambers' first year at the helm, the company had $2.2 billion in revenue and 3,000 employees. In the second half of the decade, its revenues grew steadily, reaching $8.4 billion in 1998, $12.1 billion in 1999, and $18.9 billion in 2000. Profits rose just as steadily: from $2.2 billion in 1998, to $3.2 billion in 1999, to $4.3 billion in 2000.

This was a record of growth that had rarely, if ever, been matched by other U.S. business firms. Indeed, no other major corporation rose so quickly to the top of its industry.

By virtue of its huge annual growth rates, Cisco was Wall Street's darling; Cisco was Wall Street's most heavily traded stock. The only question that seemed relevant was how high could Cisco go? John Chambers himself spoke of Cisco becoming Wall Street's first trillion-dollar market value company. When he made that pronouncement, few winced.

Right up to the winter of 2000, Chambers kept insisting that 30–50 percent annual growth rates were not merely possible, but probable for Cisco over the next five years. As it headed for a probable $30-billion revenue year in fiscal 2001, the media noted that if Cisco kept growing at a mind-boggling 40 percent a year, it would become a $110-billion company by 2005, almost as large as GE was in 2001. More astounding, it had taken GE over 100 years to get that large; John Chambers would get there in only 21!

For much of 2000, Cisco's revenues and profits soared. Indeed, since it had gone public on February 16, 1990, Cisco Systems had been growing by more than 40 percent each year save for 1998, when it grew by a "mere" 31 percent. On August 8, 2000, Cisco reported a 61 percent rise in sales to $5.72 billion for its fourth quarter for fiscal year 2000, the company's tenth straight quarter of accelerating year-over-year revenue growth.

The stock closed at $65.50 that day. Chambers was, as usual, decidedly upbeat: "We predicted five years ago that we were in the midst of a second Industrial Revolution that would determine the prosperity of companies, countries, and individuals. Today, the Internet continues to drive the strongest U.S. economy in history. We see no indications in the marketplace that the radical Internet business transformation in practices like customer service, supply-chain management, employee training, empowerment, and e-commerce that is taking place around the world today is slowing—in fact, we believe it is accelerating globally."

This was John Chambers the motivator, the visionary, the futurist at his best. He constantly spoke of revolutions, transformations, and new ways of doing things. And the obvious assumption, of course, was that Cisco Systems was on the cusp of such a revolution.

Always, Chambers measured success in terms of revenue, the great growth indicator of our corporate age. To be sure, he cared about profits, but he didn't rely on Cisco's earnings record as a sign of how strong a company it was, or how fast it was growing. He focused on Cisco's revenues to tell the growth story. Some of Cisco's financial results during this hyper-growth phase reflected a steady hand on the wheel; Cisco met Wall Street's expectations quarter after quarter, giving rise to the Street's assumption that the company would weather any storm that arose.

None of that caused John Chambers to stop fretting. Conscious that the business world can be very fragile and unreliable, John Chambers has always been one of the world's great worriers.

HEALTHY PARANOIA

Chambers worried, above all else, that Cisco's spectacular growth could grind to a halt. Frequently, he says he possesses a "healthy paranoia" that—he likes to joke—would make Intel's Andy Grove (the father of that well-known phrase) seem relaxed. He is paranoid that Cisco might get too far from its customers, too far from its employees, too far from its partners.

There seemed little reason to worry. John Chambers did a remarkable job of "growing" Cisco. When he took over as CEO in

1995, he began to change the face of the company. By dint of his strong personality, Chambers instilled in Cisco a higher purpose. Building a nimble culture, he instituted processes in all aspects of the business that were designed to ease Cisco through its remarkable growth. Indeed, it was the congruence between the Cisco culture—energetic, high-spirited, and undaunted—and the hyper-growth environment that the super-charged U.S. economy had created that gave the Cisco Systems growth engine its main impetus.

Perhaps more important than anything else, as a means to enable Cisco to penetrate even larger markets, Chambers elevated Cisco's profile, giving the once-obscure "plumber" of the Internet a new, spruced-up public persona.

Radiating a rare degree of self-confidence, even audacity, John Chambers—never was he more visionary than in this utterance—began to preach that Cisco could change the global community forever by interconnecting everything on the planet. He sought to convince everyone that Cisco could transform the way everyone communicates and could help machines communicate with a high degree of sophistication. He hoped, he said often, to change the way people live, play, work, and learn. That applied to government, education, society, and business—it applied to everyone.

PRIMED FOR GROWTH

Even before Chambers took the controls at Cisco, the company was primed for the high-speed growth track. Its original product in 1986 was the multi-protocol router, a specialized computer that provides the "plumbing" for the Internet, sorting data packets and sending the packets on their way. In time, this unique and unprecedented Cisco product would fuel the burgeoning demand for computer networking. Without Cisco routers, there would be no World Wide Web. By the year 2000, over 75 percent of all Internet traffic traveled over Cisco products, and the future looked just as rosy: With 275 million people using the Internet, the figure was expected to mushroom to 1 billion by 2005, three and one-half times more traffic, three and one-half times as much Cisco product to sell over that five-year period.

With such optimistic projections forming a basic justification for pushing the company to grow as fast as possible, Chambers seemed to have every reason in the world to remain optimistic that Cisco would just keep on growing into the foreseeable future.

The Cisco Systems story in the 1990s, especially the John Chambers years, seemed too good to be true: increasing profits, increasing revenue, increasing stock prices. Everything was heading skyward. The company seemed unable to slow down. It was in the right set of markets at the right time, and its reputation was so stellar, its products of sufficiently high quality, selling at the right price, that Cisco simply could do no wrong.

One segment of the Cisco Systems business that propelled the skyrocketing growth was Chambers' program of acquisitions. Until John Chambers joined the company in 1991, Cisco Systems had an ambivalent attitude toward acquiring other companies. For years, the businesses of Silicon Valley frowned on acquisitions, adopting the engineers' view that if a product was "not invented here," it was not worth having. Indeed, a search for acquisitions was, in the Silicon Valley culture, a sign of weakness.

That kind of corporate chauvinism had an effect on Cisco Systems as well, although Chambers' predecessor, John Morgridge, was not entirely negative toward mergers or takeovers. He had considered a number of acquisitions, but he was not entirely at ease with taking over other companies. He worried what such acquisitions might do to Cisco internally, and he seemed sympathetic to Cisco's engineers, who had a hard time understanding why the company would take on start-ups when it was pouring so many resources into its own research and development (R&D) efforts.

Though Morgridge was lukewarm to acquisitions, Chambers was not. Cisco's rarified stock value gave it the wherewithal to make offers to other firms that other companies could not possibly match.

Chambers pursued a stream of acquisitions as a way of keeping up with the market transitions that were a trademark of the high-tech industry. Chambers and his senior staff were eager to find companies that could help them offer increased bandwidth.

In the early summer of 1993, Mario Mazzola was presiding over Sunnyvale-based Crescendo's 52 employees. Mazzola, who has remained at Cisco, recalled his first tour of Cisco soon after the September 1993 acquisition, and realized that in his wildest dreams, he had not envisioned that the purchase of Crescendo would yield one of Cisco's crown jewels. Seven years later, in 2000, Cisco's switching business, thanks first and foremost to the Crescendo purchase, had become a $10-billion-a-year business. This represented almost half of Cisco's annual revenues that year.

THE CRESCENDO SUCCESS

The purchase of Crescendo set off a chain of events that eventually transformed Cisco into the leading force in networking. The Crescendo purchase validated Cisco's theory that it could introduce "cores" of technology into the company by absorbing start-ups into Cisco's culture, or better yet, its sales machine. Cisco could multiply a start-up's revenues by contributing and using its own much larger and more powerful sales and distribution teams, without slowing down the rest of Cisco. Cisco's hyper-growth forced it to fill the pipe with more and new products, usually coming from these acquisitions. These purchases also reinforced the notion held by Cisco's leading executives that any merger of equals (a la SynOptics, 3Com, etc.) would result in a collision of cultures, and a slowing down of Cisco. Case in point: Cisco's acquisition of Crescendo did not dilute Cisco's shareholders' stock, as a merger between Cisco and SynOptics would have.

Cisco's success with the Crescendo purchase opened the way for other acquisitions, especially two other companies, Kalpana and Grand Junction. With these purchases, carried out from 1993–1995, Cisco acquired the talent that would give it the switching product it required. The results were spectacular. In 1999, fully 39 percent of Cisco's $20 billion in revenues came from switching (41 percent came from routers, 13 percent from access products, and 7 percent from other products).

The acquisition strategy was in place. Cisco executives were confident that by applying that strategy on a continuing basis, they could build a product line that would meet the needs of customers who liked dealing with one vendor, and one vendor only. Cisco's acquisition strategy got a further boost as more data, graphics, and video were put on the Internet, requiring companies like Cisco to sell more routers and switches to direct the overwhelming traffic. A takeover frenzy of sorts followed as the major players spent over $6 billion from the start of 1995 to the summer of 1996 to exploit the opportunities created by the Internet.

By September 1996, Cisco had a market cap larger than $30 billion. By embarking on its acquisition strategy—scooping up 13 companies by this point—it had the broadest technology lineup of any networking supplier; its products ranged from access servers to routers and switches. Some predicted that Cisco's luck would run out and that one or more of its acquisitions would fail. But John Chambers vowed to push on, vowed to pursue six to ten more acquisitions over the next year. By that September, it had spent $5.5 billion on those 13 acquisitions.

By September, Cisco had achieved a dominant position in most of the markets in which it was engaged. It had a 72 percent market share in high-end routing. It was number 1 in LAN switching, with 35 percent of the market; in the enterprise market, it was nearing 50 percent market share with its Fast Ethernet Catalyst 5000 product. It was also number 1 in the IBM SNA/internetwork marketplace as well, with 73 percent of the market share.

Why the rush to buy all these companies, Chambers was asked? Because, the Cisco CEO suggested, for the six months before the acquisitions, customers were adopting a new strategy of using a single vendor for their network purchases. Accordingly, Cisco was trying to acquire the best-in-class products in each segment.

In 1997, Cisco's executives began to sense that a market transition was occurring and that it would be prudent to take on the data/voice/video market aggressively. As a result, Chambers planned to step up acquisitions in this field. Cisco's main competitors were Lucent and Nortel. Lucent had revenue of $38 billion in 1999; Nortel had $17.6 billion.

From 1993–1999, Cisco acquired 40 start-ups for a total of nearly $20 billion. In October 1999, John Chambers passed the word that Cisco planned to step up its dizzying pace of acquisitions and would probably buy more than 20 companies in the year, spending $10 billion in cash and stock. Until then, Cisco had bought 40 companies. It had purchased 10 alone in 1999, including Cerent. It would be going after companies in areas that dealt with voice, data, and video integration. As it had predicted, Cisco, by May 2000, had added another 15 companies—55 in all since it began its acquisition strategy, paying out $20.4 billion. That number had grown to 69 by December 2000.

To hear John Chambers tell it, Cisco had no option but to grow. Even if the Wall Street analysts were suggesting that eventually, if only because of something called the Law of Large Numbers, Cisco would not be able to grow as fast as it had been, Chambers only pretended to heed the advice. He spoke frequently of constantly feeling paranoid about how well the company was doing, and how conscious he was that one wrong step and Cisco might suffer a serious reverse.

It is to Chambers' credit that he seemed ever watchful for the signs that Cisco's bubble might be bursting. He understood that no matter how essential his products were, no matter how aggressive his sales force was, he could not automatically take growth for granted into the long-range future. Nonetheless, there is an inherent problem for companies like Cisco Systems that play the growth card. As much as they want to protect themselves against external pressures that can bring them down, the very fact that they focus on growth creates built-in obstacles for them when external pressures start to build. They acquire an expectation that they can grow forever, and managing such an expectation becomes quite challenging.

This, as you shall see, is what happened to John Chambers and Cisco Systems. It was not that he was making mistakes. It was more that he had set in motion a series of actions—call it the "Cisco growth engine"—that could not be halted quickly enough when it became necessary. For John Chambers, the growth king, was building more and more buildings, hiring more and more employees, and predicting, in true visionary fashion, that Cisco would grow at spectacular levels. Once the environment changed, as it did with spectacular speed in the winter of 2000–2001, the very leadership characteristics that had defined growth-oriented CEOs, such as an obsessive focus on top-line growth, being a visionary, being preoccupied with strategic alliances, and emphasizing new market development and growth, became obstacles to success in the changing environment.

Chambers believed all along that he would be able to manage expectations, that he would have enough warning that the economy was slowing down, that he could pull back in sufficient time on the levers of the growth machine—and in that way, Cisco would not hit the wall. He did not take into account that an economic downturn could occur suddenly, that, as he put it later, a "100-year flood" would occur, making it all but impossible for him to manage his company's expectations of hyper-growth, of dealing quickly and effectively with the flood. Some, including myself, would argue that being prepared for such an economic downturn was really a "Risk Management 101" lesson. Whether by personal understanding, coaching from his board of directors, or his communications people, Chambers has since stopped using the "100-year flood" metaphor.

The main question facing John Chambers was this: Could Cisco apply the brakes on all that growth quickly enough to enable the company to install performance-driven initiatives that would set the company right?

This is a major problem facing growth-oriented companies: How to assure that a proper balance between growth and performance is achieved, even as a company surges toward growth.

But, John Chambers found that it was easier to put the pedal to the metal than to take it off and switch over to the performance side.

Some have suggested that it was Chambers' lack of operational skills—something that had not seemed terribly important to the Cisco board of directors when it chose him to run the company—that might have been the cause for his inability to apply the brakes quickly enough.

As late as December 2000, managing the hyper-growth it was experiencing remained a major priority for Cisco. This was a company that was hiring 1,000 new employees a month. It was building new office parks and planning to more than double its then 42,000 employees to 100,000 employees over the next few years.

It was not that Chambers was unaware of the dangers that an economic downturn, characterized by a slowdown in corporate investment, might pose to Cisco. But he and his chief financial officer (CFO), Larry Carter, simply assumed that there would be sufficient warning, perhaps as much as one to two quarters, by which time Cisco would be able to take the necessary measures to take a downturn into account.

Even if John Chambers and his networked virtual organization had detected the truth about the sudden paralysis that gripped the U.S. economy in late 2000 and early 2001, the Cisco growth engine had far too much momentum to simply stop in its tracks. A company that is on a growth track, as Cisco was, cannot plan for the hiring of thousands of employees, the building of numerous campuses, and the building up of millions of dollars' worth of inventory, and then, as it were, stop on a dime. When the economic downturn occurred, Cisco tried to stop on a dime—it curtailed all of its growth-oriented initiatives—but the costs to the company, especially in terms of lost inventory, were huge.

Chambers learned all too painfully and without warning in early 2001, when a faltering economy burst the Cisco bubble, that THE SAME INGREDIENTS FOR GROWTH CAN BECOME COUNTERPRODUCTIVE, OR EVEN THE SEEDS OF DISASTER, IN A DOWN MARKET.

A WEAKENED ECONOMY

Late in 2000, the U.S. economy suddenly went into a tailspin and company after company ran into trouble. At first, Chambers thought Cisco could ride out the storm, but by early 2001, the vaunted Cisco Systems was reeling as customer after customer stopped ordering. Planning for continued growth, Cisco had built up huge inventories. What would happen to those inventories? Was it possible that employees might have to be laid off?

Though he had vowed that he would quit before laying off employees, John Chambers found that in March 2001, he had no choice but to lay off 7,900 employees. He was forced to write off billions of dollars of inventory. The swaggering stock plummeted. Cisco Systems was no longer the growth king. John Chambers stopped making assertions about the lofty promise of the Internet.

ACHIEVING STRATEGIC CALIBRATION

Executives who have figured out how to grow their companies have had to learn as well how to focus on and drive efficiencies, and how to meet short-term expectations. The temptation, of course, is to keep after the growth-oriented projects and not pay attention to the performance side of the business. Achieving that kind of strategic recalibration can be extremely difficult for growth-oriented firms.

The test is not whether a company that has been doing exceedingly well can avoid setbacks. Everyone stumbles. It would be unfair to hold Cisco Systems to such a high standard. But clearly, Cisco reflects the glories and perils of embarking and relying entirely on a growth-oriented strategy.

It was time for John Chambers to try to break through the wall. He would attempt to strategically recalibrate Cisco by focusing more on the performance side. He called it, "going back to the basics." He also put a new emphasis on what he called "FOCUS AND EXECUTION."

More than anything else, Chambers would have to demonstrate to shareholders and the media that the company could manage very well even when hyper-growth was no longer possible. While Chambers had been able to manage expectations very well quarter after quarter, year after year, Cisco's setbacks left outsiders with a feeling that the company was no longer in control of its future. Chambers had to find a way to convince others that the company was in control, and the path he chose was to recalibrate the company's strategies.

His goal was to get Cisco back on financial track as quickly as possible, to return to those days of quarter-after-quarter growth, to reach a time again when Wall Street could develop the same kind of positive expectations that it had held toward the company in earlier years.

ENGAGING IN STRATEGIC RECALIBRATION

Faster than most other CEOs, Chambers realized that Cisco required major reforms. He undertook a six-point plan early in 2001 that, among other things, put a new stress on profits, froze expenses, especially new hires, and required a new effort at teamwork.

Due to the downturn in its fortunes, the company was forced to focus on fewer market opportunities. Chambers exerted a sizable effort to realign Cisco's resources. He planned to take a close look at under-performing units within the company and elimi-

nate them, where necessary; acquisitions that were not producing new, viable products would be the first to go. Finally, he
undertook a vast company-wide reorganization. Before the reorganization, business units were segmented by customer type.
After the reorganization, they were structured by technology.

No longer would revenue growth be exalted; earnings would be
emphasized. No longer would Cisco pile on employee after
employee, campus after campus. Indeed, Chambers gave a new
priority to TALENT MANAGEMENT. He hired Kate DCamp, as his
new vice president for human resources. Kate, who had worked
for years at GE, and whose style was no-nonsense, brought a
fresh mandate to make sure that employees were as productive
as possible. In addition to such key hires, he shifted other talent
around: Mario Mazzola, who had come over to Cisco in the Crescendo acquisition, was put in charge of all engineering efforts.
Mike Volpi, the company's top strategist, was given more operational responsibilities. Twenty percent of Cisco's engineers were
given new jobs in areas of higher priority.

New emphasis was put on finding leadership potential from
within the existing employe base. The goal was to create a fast-
track program to promote certain employees faster than ever.

The recruitment process was overhauled. In the few years before
the setback, Cisco hired in volume, bringing in thousands of
employees a year. At the time, its officials insisted that it was
taking in only the best. Let's get real, that would have been
impossible. I don't care how good an HR organization you have,
when a company of 10,000 people is hiring 3,000 people per
quarter, you're not bringing in all A-players. And after the setbacks, senior executives acknowledged that the high-volume hiring had allowed a number of people to get in who probably
should not have been hired. The company had such a high
demand for employees that it could not do a perfect job in select-
ing and integrating the thousands it was taking in each year. New

recruits were expected to sink or swim on their own. With volume hiring a thing of the past, Cisco began looking for a "few good employees."

Specifically, John Chambers' plan called for these six new priorities: slowing head count growth and discretionary spending, aligning resources with major growth opportunities, focusing on profit contribution (rather than revenues), leveraging e-applications to gain productivity, ensuring that everyone focused on their own areas of improvement, and remaining focused on Cisco's breakaway strategy. If there was a common theme to the six-point plan, it was that Cisco would jettison its growth strategy for the time being, and put a major focus on performance-oriented initiatives that would improve the company's balance sheet.

Because Cisco could no longer rely on growth as the main stimulant for the company's success, it had to move over to the left side of the portfolio framework and stress business fundamentals such as discipline and rigor, profit, and productivity. These fundamentals were needed to deal with the brand-new business environment for Cisco. Gone were the halcyon days when hyper-growth opportunities existed in numerous markets. Some of those markets had simply disappeared overnight after a heady, promising start. Nowhere was this truer than in the telecommunications market, where start-up after start-up promised new ways to bring voice, data, and video together, and then failed to deliver mostly because the market wasn't yet ripe. And their debt load was suffocating them.

Some questioned whether Chambers had applied the brakes swiftly enough at the time of the downturn, and whether he could drive the performance side adequately. His biggest challenge was to switch from hyper-growth—40 percent annual growth rates—to efforts at cost control and productivity, the kind of efforts that would restore the company to profitability.

Some questioned whether Chambers could go from being a cheerleader to a disciplinarian. Could he put aside the meetings with political leaders and speeches to Internet conferences and focus instead on steering Cisco through the severe economic downturn?

SIGN OF RECOVERY

The first concrete sign of recovery was less the news that Cisco had posted third-quarter sales for fiscal 2002 of $4.822 billion, just a slight bit up from the previous quarter; rather, it was the announcement that company profits had been $729 million, a 10 percent quarter-over-quarter growth. It was this consistency of effort that pleased John Chambers and Wall Street alike. Strategic recalibration seemed to be working.

That news sent Cisco's stock up 24 percent on May 8, 2002, to $16.27, adding more than $20 billion to Cisco's market cap. The positive financial figures from Cisco gave NASDAQ its eighth largest percentage gain ever, 7.8 percent.

On August 6, 2002, Cisco produced largely heartening results for its fourth quarter for fiscal 2002. Its net sales for that final quarter were $4.8 billion, up 12 percent over the fourth quarter of a year earlier ($4.3 billion). Its net income was even more astonishing: $772 million for the final quarter, compared to $7 for the final quarter the year before.

Fiscal 2002 revenues came to $18.9 billion, down 15 percent from the fiscal 2001 figure of $22.3 billion. It was on the earnings side that Cisco reflected the recovery for which Chambers had been striving: fiscal earnings were $1.9 billion compared to a net loss of $1 billion for the year before. Cisco had $21.5 billion on hand at the end of the year.

On the day that Cisco reported those final quarter figures, Chambers noted, "Throughout this challenging time, we have focused on four key areas: profits, cash generation, productivity, and profitable market share gains. We have consistently improved quarter by quarter in each of these categories, with our fourth quarter bringing in more than $1 billion in pro forma net income, $1.6 billion in cash from operations, a 22 percent productivity increase over last year's fourth quarter, and 12 percent year-over-year revenue growth compared to a 44 percent decline by our top ten competitors."

Chambers believed that as long as the company could continue to turn in consistently good quarters, bouncing back especially on the profit side, Cisco would truly be headed for a return, if not to the great glory days of the recent past, then at least to days when everyone could smile.

The CEO was taking into account that creating a performance-based culture would take time. So much of Cisco had been about growth. Now, Chambers was trying to steer the company in a different direction, being more careful—still taking risks, but making sure to take only the most calculated ones.

He was also talking a lot about the need to get more productive. He wanted to see Cisco employees get more productive, and he wanted to see the U.S. economy get more productive. If both did, he was sure that Cisco would once again do just fine.

Cisco's earnings surged 50 percent in the second fiscal quarter of 2003; it earned $991 million on sales of $4.7 billion. In the same quarter last year, the company earned $660 million on sales of $4.8 billion. Sales for the first six months of fiscal 2003 were $9.6 billion, compared with $9.3 billion for the first six months of fiscal 2002, an increase of 3.2 percent.

Chambers was essentially satisfied with Cisco's performance. "In what is probably the most challenging environment the information technology industry has ever faced, we are very pleased with our results in posting one of the best pro forma quarters in our history and the best GAAP [generally accepted accounting principles] quarter in terms of net income and earnings per share. Our market performance reflects Cisco's ability to deliver differentiated value to our customers' highest priority—productivity."

Still, there was still no clear indication when things would turn around for Cisco: Growth, for Cisco, lies on several fronts, two of which are the telecommunications market, which is still reeling, and the consumer market, where Cisco has struggled and where the margins are anemic. Its recent acquisition of Linksys should help liven up its consumer business and make for some interesting times ahead.

In looking at the kinds of things that executives use to bring their companies out of the doldrums, the focus thus far has been on certain areas that fall under the leadership category. The next chapter will deal with another area where executives can engage themselves in the quest for breaking through the wall: governance.

HOW TO PLAY
THE GAME

5

GOVERNANCE: TOUGH RULES FOR TOUGH TIMES

THE RUTHLESS EXECUTION CHECKLIST

1. Are you relentless about linking incentives to results rather than activities?

2. Do you effectively analyze and prioritize initiatives/investments?

3. Do you regularly kill/close non-performing initiatives?

4. Do you regularly review and validate the operational measure you manage by?

5. Do you enforce accountability for deliverables, and are the consequences real?

So far this book has covered in detail the first of the three strategies that business leaders need to employ to break through the wall: LEADERSHIP.

In this chapter, we will discuss the second critical strategy: GOVERNANCE. It is important to note that although the whole notion of governance is structural in nature, the elements found within this concept set boundaries for action. By governance, I mean operational governance rather than corporate governance, which proliferates today's business news.

Focusing on the rules of the game that govern how leaders should execute, these rules embrace three important elements: accountability, performance management, and discipline.

In the leadership strategy section, we saw that business leaders decided what strategies should be employed to induce business recovery. With the governance strategy, leaders frame the rules of the game (accountability, performance management system, and discipline) before they put those strategies into practice.

ACCOUNTABILITY

To overcome business reversals, business leaders must develop a strong system of ACCOUNTABILITY. They must not only know what tasks to assign, they must assure that their senior colleagues take responsibility for getting those tasks implemented efficiently, speedily, and precisely as designed. And most important, they must deliver results.

NOTHING IS MORE IMPORTANT TO A SMOOTHLY RUN ORGANIZATION THAN HAVING A SOLID SYSTEM OF ACCOUNTABILITY. By accountability, I mean not just personal accountability, but accountability that deals with the greater good of the company—moving away from what's good for my particular part of the business to what is best for the overall company. THIS IS SOMETHING THAT BUSINESS LEADERS STRUGGLE WITH THE MOST. MOST EVERY BUSINESS LEADER USES THE "TEAM" WORD IN THEIR RHETORIC. BUT TO TRULY GET SENIOR LEADERSHIP TO THINK AND ACT FOR IMPROVED SHAREHOLDER VALUE, EVEN AT THE EXPENSE OF HIS OR HER OWN AREA, IS THE CHALLENGE.

Accountability is nothing more than making good on one's commitments, goals, and targets, and dealing with the consequences if one does not keep those commitments. This might sound "ruthless," but when this message is effectively communicated, as it was with the leaders I studied, it will come off sounding fair and clear, and will be respected by the greater organization.

Holding colleagues accountable requires the right kind of ALIGNMENT across a whole spectrum of relationships inside and outside the company. One person who understands this point is Harry Kraemer. I will devote an entire chapter later to his leadership of Baxter International. Harry provided the right kind of incentives to his executives to help make sure their focus was on Baxter and not themselves. Those incentives assured that the executives were aligned with each part of the business. For Kraemer, creating the right kind of alignment was a crucial step on the road to an effective system of accountability.

One important way to have accountability is to assure that all elements of the company are on the same page. For business leaders who figured out how to recover from reversals, it was terribly important to create an alignment with employees, share-holders, Wall Street, and the media. Creating the right kind of alignment means that those outside and inside the business KNOW PRECISELY WHAT THE COMPANY IS DOING AND WHY AT ANY GIVEN TIME. Proper alignment—a critical element in getting through business difficulties—is the result of business leaders and executives COMMUNICATING MESSAGES CONSISTENTLY to the various forces, messages having to do with the company's goals, its prospects, and its challenges.

THE NOTION OF ALIGNMENT

Alignment represents all those efforts by which a business leader makes sure that the company is working in harmony, functioning smoothly and efficiently. In short, management and employees are operating in tandem and in alignment with business strategies.

It is very important for executives trying to align employees, shareholders, the media, etc. to be very PRECISE and consistent at all times. Accordingly, CONSISTENT COMMUNICATIONS are crucial in attempting to set a company right after a reversal.

It is fundamentally the responsibility of the business leaders to drive organizational alignment (for the overall corporation, it's the CEO and CFO; for the business unit or function, it is the senior business leader). But, it is by no means easy. While most CEOs make painstaking efforts at organizational alignment, translating this strategy into effective action and execution is a huge challenge.

When the CEO falters, the company's board may step in and decide whether to make a change at the top. The board must make a very delicate but crucial decision on whether to stick with the CEO. After all, it is the CEO who has led the company into the recent setback. Perhaps he or she should go? Perhaps the company wants to start fresh?

The only true measure of whether a CEO should be allowed to continue is whether he or she still has the trust and loyalty of customers, investors, and employees. In some cases, that is hard to determine, but in others, it can be determined very quickly. When Cisco Systems suffered a serious reversal of fortune in the winter of 2000–2001, Cisco's board gave an immediate vote of confidence to CEO John Chambers. In doing so, it was signaling that the board did not blame Chambers personally for the calamity; it blamed forces within the U.S. economy over which the CEO could not possibly have had control.

When a CEO does not enjoy the support of customers, investors, and employees, as well as the board of directors, it is wisest to remove the CEO before undertaking any steps toward recovery. It took very little to convince the IBM board that John Akers had to go in 1993 since the company had been bleeding billions of dollars. Because Akers had lost the confidence of just about everyone around him, getting rid of him was an easy decision.

WANTED: LEADERSHIP COMMITMENT

The same goes for the senior leadership team. For these strategies and practices to be truly effective, the senior leadership team must be committed. If not, it would be best to replace those who aren't with others who will be.

We have been addressing the issue of accountability, which begs the question: How can one guarantee that executives will feel the need to be accountable? That brings us to our next practice under governance, the performance management system.

PERFORMANCE MANAGEMENT SYSTEM

If accountability is about making good on one's promises, goals, and targets, the single best way to make sure that employees are accountable is to have in place the best possible system for measuring results. Just as a company must have a smoothly working accountability system to break through a wall, it is just as critical that it have an effective performance management system.

A proper performance management system helps employees learn what is important, how tasks are to be measured, and how those tasks affect the overall business enterprise. It can become an effective tool for aligning management and employees as they seek to attain targeted goals. It can show business leaders how to go from broad strategies to day-to-day actions. It can transmit a company's strategies not just to the top leadership, but throughout the company.

An effective performance management system helps communicate goals and strategies, providing management the understanding to create a true performance-focused organization. It permits business leaders to measure actual performance against the full potential of their businesses.

Research indicates that companies with strong performance management systems do better than their peers.

What performance management systems should be used to deal with rude awakenings in your business? Most companies in the past have determined their financial progress by looking at benchmarks such as sales, margins, profit, and market value. But to truly judge the strategic welfare of a company, you need performance management systems that reflect the entire strategy of the company—how customers look at the value proposition.

RESULTS OR BUST

Unfortunately, most companies' strategic priorities were often entirely separated from the way employees were evaluated and the tasks those employees were asked to perform. As a result, companies frequently devised performance measures that had no impact on a company's financial results. Numerous activities were measured and simply became substitutes for results.

The business leaders I studied have done whatever it takes to avoid a situation in which they have had to explain away bad results. They learned that they had to put in place reward and incentive systems that helped to ensure that employees would deliver on what mattered to the company. An effective performance management system makes sure that results get delivered and that the results are for the good of the company.

An effective system of performance measurement requires:

1. Identifying and correctly measuring critical business functions.

2. Planning business activities with operating measurements in mind.

3. Creating a technical capability that will gather, store, and support the measurement process.

Most companies struggle constantly with performance measurement. They create performance management systems that are overly complicated. An effective system must be simple, transparent, and uniform, one that will greatly aid others in understanding your company's strategies, and truly reflect how the company creates value.

ALL MEASURES ARE NOT CREATED EQUAL

Business leaders often do not differentiate between using different kinds of performance measures, and they should.

METRIC DISCRIMINATION

Business leaders should not use the same kinds of measures to gauge different kinds of business initiatives. For example, they use certain measures to track growth activity and other measures for activities designed simply to run the business.

The performance portfolio framework shown in Figure 5–1 depicts how business leaders should discriminate between various performance measures. For example, some measures are much more appropriate when you are in a growth mode than when you are in a performance mode. And sometimes there are measures available but not used that can provide valuable insight. Cisco is a good example; at its peak, it was focusing on top-line revenue growth and gross margins. These are examples of the kinds of performance measures that seem reasonable to watch when a company is in hyper-growth mode. But, by paying attention to the increasing debt of its rivals and telcos (telecommunication companies), and the reduction in Internet traffic growth, Cisco could have gained some warning that growth was about to stall . . . .

FIGURE 5–1
Performance portfolio framework.

WALKING THE TIGHTROPE

The measurement problem is typically bi-modal. Companies tend to either measure the right things but don't do a good job of actually measuring and tracking; or they measure too many things, many of which aren't relevant. This is a delicate balancing act.

Some business initiatives lend themselves to easily quantifiable measures such as cost savings. Others rely on revenue and profit growth, especially those initiatives that cover new markets or incremental revenue opportunities. Still others are measured by non-financial factors such as improved customer experience, better customer-facing processes, and increasing the value of a product or service to the customer.

A performance management system must be context-specific: The business leader first decides what business initiative to undertake, and then makes sure there is an appropriate mechanism to review and track that initiative.

On the performance side, measures should be much more attuned to short-term revenue growth (e.g., return on invested capital). The left-hand side of the portfolio framework lends itself better to traditional kinds of performance measures: It includes discounted cash flow analysis and ROI calculations.

As for right-hand-side growth initiatives, ROI measures simply don't work. Breakthroughs and rational experimentation often deal with emerging investments, where the disparity between the potential upside and downside is large, future revenues are highly uncertain, and initial investments are relatively small compared to the requisite future investments of scaling fully. Time horizons are longer than usual.

While companies would never play fast and loose with performance measures when it comes to their core business, they often take a nonchalant view of performance measurement when it comes to the growth side. Many business leaders tend to be less rigorous when it comes to measuring growth efforts. Why is that?

One reason is that EXECUTIVES INTERESTED IN GROWTH PROJECTS TEND TO CHANGE STRATEGIES SO RAPIDLY that it becomes too difficult to think of either a long-term strategy or a measure that follows from the strategy. Another reason is that MEASUREMENT IS RESOURCE-INTENSIVE. Acquiring performance measurement data sometimes requires large amounts of capital investment and human resources. Finally, executives interested in growth-oriented initiatives tend to RELY ON MEASURES THAT ARE SOFT; HOWEVER, THE INVESTMENT COMMUNITY DOES NOT PUT MUCH VALUE IN SOFT MEASURES. Wall Street has had a high comfort level with hard numbers—revenues and margins—but, when it comes to the softer measures dealing with things such as customer perception, these data are not so highly valued.

Executives engaged in right-hand-side business now express financial performance not so much in terms of GAAP measures (which focus on present-period costs and revenues), but more on prospective valuations that reflect growth platforms.

With regard to performance management, the key principles used by successful business leaders whom I studied were:

- **PRINCIPLE 1**—They focus on a select few performance measurements and take great care not to dilute the need for focus with too many measures. It is critical to find measures that matter to the business. Ask yourself what is the total number of metrics you and your managers track. How many of those metrics are truly relevant to shareholder value?

- **PRINCIPLE 2**—They believe that an unusually broad set of measures slows down execution and complicates rather than clarifies the critical managerial discussions and decision-making required. To these leaders, driving shareholder value is their number one priority. All other measures come second.

- **PRINCIPLE 3**—They prefer certain operating measures, such as top-line revenue growth, cash flow, working capital reduction, and return on invested capital, as the key performance indicators that will drive shareholder value.

- **PRINCIPLE 4**—They are relentless about determining what performance measures truly matter and make sure that those performance measures are linked to the strategic priorities of the company. Unfortunately, as you move down in an organization, you will find that often over 50 percent of the metrics being used have little relevance to company results.

- **PRINCIPLE 5**—They prefer performance measurement systems that are disciplined and rigorous. A system is disciplined when the measurement and review processes are applied consistently and fairly on a regular basis and that "gaming the system" is minimized.

- **PRINCIPLE 6**—They make a habit of revisiting these performance measurements every few years to prevent them from getting stale or becoming obsolete. It is amazing how long leaders can go without truly questioning the currency and relevance of the numbers they manage by.

- **PRINCIPLE 7**—Because they are fact-based in their approach to performance measurement, they are comfortable setting stretch goals. In most companies, target setting is a joke.

- **PRINCIPLE 8**—They have a clear focus on what business initiatives really matter and only measure results.

- **PRINCIPLE 9**—They are careful not to employ performance measures and targets blindly across the business.

- **PRINCIPLE 10**—They adopt measures that are very actionable, clearly and easily communicated across the organization—and most important—controllable and relevant to peoples' day-to-day activities.

In deciding how and why to allocate resources to the four quadrants of the portfolio framework, it makes sense to account for differences in terms of risk, payback period, and return type, as shown in Table 5–1.

In summary, there are good reasons for business leaders to build strong performance measurement systems as part of their recovery efforts. If those systems are clear and precise, they can help align individual objectives, departmental functional goals, and company-wide strategic efforts.

TABLE 5–1 Risk/Reward Calibrator

PORTFOLIO TYPE	RISK	PAYBACK PERIOD	RETURN TYPE
NEW FUNDAMENTALS	Low	3–12 months	SG&A (sales, general and administrative)
OPERATIONAL EXCELLENCE	Medium to high	12–24 months	Margin; working capital improvement
RATIONAL EXPERIMENTATION	Low	12–36 months	New revenue; growth
BREAKTHROUGH STRATEGIES	Medium to high	12–24 months	Revenue growth and shareholder value

DISCIPLINE

In addition to effective accountability and performance management systems, business leaders have found that discipline is an important "rule of the game" in bouncing back from business reversals.

Discipline means, above all else, knowing what has to be done, and making sure it gets done with consistency and rigor. For companies that are not mature, this is a difficult transition.

In subsequent chapters, I will discuss two business leaders at length: Lou Gerstner of IBM and Larry Bossidy of AlliedSignal, later Honeywell. These two leaders stand as models of great masters of business discipline.

It is business discipline that these two business leaders—Lou Gerstner and Larry Bossidy—understood better than most. It is why they were able to emerge from business reversals so successfully.

Discipline is all about getting results. Discipline drives consistency, the timeliness of decisions, and the institutionalizing of a formal process. In these ways, discipline is tied to performance management.

Executives who want to drive discipline through the organization had better be disciplined themselves. Employees aren't going to mind working in a disciplined manner, but they have no incentive to work hard, to work creatively, or to work efficiently if they find that the boss is not.

Rigor is important to the whole notion of discipline. TO BE RIG-OROUS and establish discipline, there must be a system of rewards and consequences that is based on facts and analytical depth.

THE DISCIPLINE OF CAPITAL INVESTMENT

"The budget is the bane of corporate America . . . . Making a budget is an exercise in minimilization. You're always trying to get the lowest out of your people . . . ," Jack Welch (*Fortune*, May 1995)

Inextricably tied to effective strategic recalibration and the performance management system of companies, is everyone's favorite annual exercise, the budget process. It is amazing how long companies force their people to spend on an activity that is so dreaded (for a company of any reasonable size, it is not uncommon for this process to take six months or more). From my vantage point, anything over 60 days is obscene. Nonetheless, most organizations have a budgeting process that is fraught with problems:

■ The capital investment process often breeds a sense of entitlement throughout the organization. It encourages "use it or lose it" behavior, which forces poor decision making for fear of not getting unused funds back.

■ The calendar and financial focus of the process inhibits the understanding of performance issues.

■ The typically centralized effort encourages resource silos and binds those resources to particular organizations rather than allowing them to move to new priorities.

FROM CAPITAL MANAGEMENT TO STRATEGIC INVESTMENT

It is squarely on the shoulders of the CFO to fix these issues. More than anyone else, the CFO holds the key to linking the strategic planning and recalibration effort and the capital and resource allocation process. Companies that excel at this lean toward a more frequent and shorter effort, which provide them with more accurate forecasts and a more flexible allocation of funds.

■ The procedure is typically long on process and details and short of valuable information business leaders require to run the business.

■ The yearly effort and the allocation process does not leave room for priorities or opportunities that come up during off-cycle periods, and many investment/project opportunities are indeed off-cycle.

STRIVING FOR CONSISTENCY

Smart business executives, in their quest for discipline, need to reward the kind of behavior that contributes to the results they are seeking. If it's teamwork that is being sought, then reward team performance, not individual performance. If it's superior customer service, don't reward volume and nothing else.

Establishing discipline does not mean punishing every employee who makes a mistake. Employees should be permitted to make mistakes without the bosses coming down on them harshly each time. Achieving desired results may require experimentation, gambling on something not tried before. So, mistakes are going to occur. They are inevitable. Think of any employee who makes mistakes as gaining the kind of experience that prevents mistakes in the future. That's a kind of discipline, too.

Nothing is more important than BEING CONSISTENT in passing on messages. Employees are going to search hard for reasons not to make the extra effort that leads to sought-after results. No one wants to waste time and effort. So, consistent messaging avoids the impression that management has no idea what to do.

I am not alone in my research findings that indicates the need for business executives to work hard at discipline. Jim Collins, the author of *Good to Great, Why Some Companies Make the Leap . . . and Others Don't* (New York: HarperCollins, 2001), one of the most popular business books of the era, concluded after his research that there was no magic formula to guarantee a company's success. Collins and his research team found that successful enterprises did not need high-profile CEOs, or the latest technology, or even great business strategies. What they needed above all was a culture that searched zealously for disciplined employees and promoted staffers who thought and acted in a disciplined manner. As noted earlier, acting in a disciplined manner means being able to get the job done, and get it done quickly, efficiently, and without ensnaring others in a bureaucratic maze.

But, even knowing how to execute does not guarantee that companies will be able to impose discipline easily. Companies, especially those that are doing well, find it hard to rein in employees who have been told that the main goal of the company is to grow.

One company that found it hard to drive discipline was Cisco Systems. As long as Cisco was growing throughout the 1990s, there seemed little reason for it to be very disciplined. As mentioned in the previous chapter, in the winter of 2000–2001, the economy suddenly turned sour and the company suffered a serious setback. Orders virtually stopped. The company stopped growing. At first, Cisco Systems' John Chambers saw no value in imposing discipline because he didn't believe that he or his company had done anything wrong. But later, after gaining some detachment, he concluded that his company needed important reform. He undertook a major shift of strategic priorities, helping Cisco to recover far more quickly than most expected. He decided to behave in a no-nonsense, demanding manner; he decided to impose discipline on his company.

For Chambers and Cisco Systems, imposing discipline was no easy feat because it is often difficult for relatively young companies in a go-go mode to tone down the pace. There are definite advantages to having plenty of cash, to being market-dominant, and to maintaining 60 percent plus operating margins, especially in economic downturns. But, the downside to having lots of cash and 60 percent operating margins is that you can hide a lot of garbage. And so, transitioning from those heady days to times when one must be focused, more attuned to working capital, and disciplined does not happen overnight. It's not impossible to accomplish, but it does not come easy. And it did not come easy to Cisco.

We have seen that the three elements mentioned prominently in this chapter—accountability, performance management, and discipline—are the building blocks with respect to governance. However, COMMITMENT and COMPLIANCE are essential for the new rules of the game to work. By commitment, I mean up and down buy-in to the new rules of the game. By compliance, I mean actual conformity and adherence to the new rules. Everyone must be on-board, especially the senior leadership team. This is something that was made clear to me by Office Depot's CEO, Bruce Nelson.

The first case study in the area of governance will tell of a man who decided that the only way to help his company through its near-calamitous crisis was to impose new discipline and rigor on its business processes. The only question was: Would that discipline and rigor assure his company's survival?

6

THE EXECUTIONER: LOU GERSTNER IMPOSES A NEW DISCIPLINE AT IBM

Lou Gerstner, the man who took over IBM in 1993, a perilous time for Big Blue when it was floundering, exemplifies the notion of discipline better than anyone else in U.S. business.

When Gerstner joined IBM on April 1, 1993, the board of directors asked him to focus on a single short-term objective: saving the company. He admitted afterwards that, given his limited knowledge of the company, he had no way of knowing whether that could be done, or how long it might take.

Gerstner saved the day by realizing that the problem IBM had been suffering from over the years had nothing to do with the quality of its products, but with the agonizing fact that THE MAN-AGEMENT HAD NOT BEEN IMPOSING A SUFFCIENT AMOUNT OF DISCIPLINE WITHIN THE ORGANIZATION.

He decided that the company needed to be rigorous in executing its initiatives, and it had to be consistent: All parts of the company had to embrace Gerstner's way of doing business, all the time. That was, in his view, how one became consistent.

During the 1980s and early 1990s, IBM was on the verge of a major crisis. It was turning out excellent products, but it fell down on the execution side. All those years of success had created inertia and complacency, indeed, an arrogance that kept IBM from responding successfully to market innovation.

When Gerstner got ready to retire early in 2002, IBM had become a service-heavy business that was the envy of the computer industry. It had regained leadership in a number of key markets where it had once lagged: servers, software, and storage devices. By late 2000, the high-tech industry was in serious trouble and was experiencing a downturn that continued for several years. However, IBM was able to hold revenues relatively stable through the slump and well outperformed its peers.

Gerstner made TWO DECISIONS that proved critical to IBM's breaking through the wall. The first was more of a non-decision: HE REVERSED THE PLAN TO BREAK UP THE COMPANY. THE SECOND WAS TO MAKE A LARGE STRATEGIC GAMBLE ON THE SERVICES BUSINESS, moving the company away from its heritage as a maker of mainframes and PCs. In 2001, IBM Global

Services was the fastest-growing segment of the company, with 42 percent of sales.

IMPOSING DISCIPLINE

The key decision that Gerstner made was to invoke A NEW STYLE WITHIN IBM, one that imposed DISCIPLINE at all levels of the organization.

Gerstner set an example by not wasting time chatting about things other than the business. He traveled frequently to learn what customers were thinking. He learned to focus on the main issues. He prided himself on being personally disciplined and hoped that the message would get through to all others at the company.

LEADING COMPUTER COMPANY

Few U.S. companies are as intriguing as IBM. For years, it was the leading company of the computer industry. It appeared invulnerable.

From 1980 to 1989, IBM made $51 billion—the most money made after taxes of any other company in the world. Its market capitalization climbed to $62.4 billion by 1990, making in the most valuable company in the U.S. That same year, it was the most profitable company on the *Fortune 500* ($5.987 billion), with revenues reaching $69 billion.

IBM appeared to know how to do it all: make the best products, and send out the best sales force into the field. Customers could not get enough of IBM technology. The conventional wisdom within U.S. business was that no one got fired for purchasing IBM equipment.

Riding so high, IBM shocked nearly everyone by its failure to perform, especially in the late 1980s and early 1990s. What had happened?

The slide was gradual. It is not possible to point to any single moment or event that started IBM's fall from market leadership. Its leaders adopted a view toward customers that came off as arrogant, and with no one in charge able to make the tough decisions required to lead the company to success, a complacency seeped into IBM's ranks that appeared to spell disaster.

IBM employees insisted that only they knew what products to sell and how to bring them to market. By endorsing mainframes over the newly developing personal computers (PCs), these same leaders missed out on the most significant revolution in the computer industry at the time.

Being disciplined meant asking key questions such as: Did it make sense to rely on hardware when the business environment was changing? Did it not make more sense for IBM to shift in a big way into the services dimension, since consumers were increasingly crying for help with their computer needs?

But few at the top understood that a disciplined company should be giving more weight to other product lines besides mainframes, that it should be moving into the services field full steam ahead.

Another sad truth pervaded IBM's once-acclaimed go-go culture. Its sales force had grown weary of making calls. It was spending far less time in the field holding customers' hands. Yet no one felt any urgency about getting the sales force to work harder. No one at the top thought of imposing the kind of discipline that would make the sales force perform effectively.

Meanwhile, IBM's customers picked up on the new, lethargic IBM and complained bitterly that it had become too difficult to work with the IBM staff.

HEADING FOR TROUBLE

By the end of 1991, IBM was heading for serious trouble. The previous six years had resulted in IBM dropping market share in its product lines from 30 to 19 percent (one percentage point equaled $3 billion in annual revenues). Its market cap had recently dropped $18 billion. The company was growing at only a 6.6 percent annual rate. While it was still the most profitable company in the world, its profits were falling. In 1990, the company had earned $5.9 billion on $68.9 billion in revenue. But that $5.9 billion figure was in fact 10 percent less than IBM had made in 1984 on only $46 billion in revenue. While the company had $64.7 billion in revenues in 1991, astonishingly, it had lost $598 million that year.

Things kept getting worse.

Though the company's 1992 revenues were $64.5 billion, IBM had lost money for the second straight year, this time, a remarkable $6.8 billion. Some 117,000 IBM employees lost their jobs; the company had to write off over $28 billion in restructuring costs.

Had there been a business leader willing to impose discipline, he or she probably would have given IBM a new lease on life, but its executives could not do what was needed: bring to an end the "job for life" policy that had been an anchor of the company's culture. The bureaucracy had swelled to 407,000 employees by 1986. The costs in salaries alone were enormous. Knife-wielding seemed in order.

Yet, while IBM contended that it had cut its work force by more than 80,000 employees from 1986 to 1992, the fact was that those reductions came through attrition, not outright dismissals. Unable to drop its no-layoff policy, IBM executed gently, not in a disciplined way.

The gentleness of IBM's chief executive, John Akers, created the illusion that Big Blue was getting its house in order. In fact, the company remained big and its costs remained high.

Rather than embark on corporate re-engineering, by the early 1990s, IBM came up with a plan to split the enterprise into a loosely federated group of businesses. Akers thought the new entities would become leaner and faster. Few could believe that the enterprise that Tom Watson, Sr. created was about to be chopped into small pieces.

As the plan went forward early in 1993, the IBM board decided to find a new CEO. It was not as if the board felt that a new CEO might help the company recover; it was more that the board of directors wanted John Akers to go. Under his leadership, the company was losing billions of dollars.

Lou Gerstner was chosen to replace Akers. His arrival marked the first time that IBM had selected an outsider to lead the company. Prior to joining IBM, Gerstner spent four years as chairman and CEO of RJR Nabisco, a huge snack food and cigarette company, and he had spent 11 years as a senior executive at American Express prior to that. He had acquired a reputation as a superb corporate turnaround artist. While at RJR Nabisco, he cut costs aggressively, reducing RJR's debt from $29 billion to $14 billion during his tenure.

Gerstner joined IBM at a time when the company had reported an $8.1-billion loss. Smaller, nimbler competitors had learned to compete ruthlessly for customers, and accordingly were licking Big Blue in all of its businesses. Customers had become smarter, demanding better products at lower prices; they were jumping the IBM ship as fast as employees. The pace of technological change in the early 1990s was relentless; it seemed as though it would be mission-impossible for the lethargic, arrogant IBM to play catch-up. Wall Street analysts thought Gerstner's best move was to simply implement the splitting up of IBM and then sell the pieces.

KEEPING IBM TOGETHER

In perhaps his most important decision throughout his nearly nine years running IBM, Gerstner decided right off the bat that he would not split up IBM. Instead, he chose to rebuild IBM. He believed that IBM's strength was its size and each segment would gain by being linked to the others. Many inside IBM and out favored the break-up, but Gerstner wanted the company to become more integrated and become the one technology company that could do almost anything—in a disciplined way.

He exploited his role as an outsider, examining every nook and cranny of IBM with a fresh, bottom-line approach. He did not go for the home run; he threw no "Hail, Mary" passes. There would be no mega-merger, no splitting of IBM, nor did he plan to articulate a vision. "Methodical" and "plodding" became his bywords.

Plenty of people believed that only a miracle could save IBM, and so they assumed that Gerstner had a miracle up his sleeve. What was his vision? they asked him repeatedly, until he finally grew weary of the question, suggesting that the last thing IBM needed was another vision. He believed in good hard work, keeping costs in line, getting the sales force to refamiliarize itself with customers, and taking a tough, hard look at which IBM businesses were performing and which were not. He saw virtue in the mainframe market but refused to overlook the newly emergent PC segment.

Of course, it was not so simple. IBM had long been dependent on profit from its mainframes, but that market was shrinking quickly. Sales of PCs—where profit margins were only half those of mainframes—had not made up the difference.

He believed that GRAND VISIONS WERE OF NO USE; they were no more than words on paper. Who could afford the time for long-term plans and strategies when IBM was suffering such short-term deficiencies? In his view, he had little option but to focus on the present. Perhaps, if all went well, if IBM managed to put its house in order, if the bottom line showed steady improvement, then he might be able to deal with a grand vision. Gerstner knew he had his critics, particularly Wall Street analysts and the media. Both argued that he could not lead IBM successfully without a vision; but their words fell on deaf ears. Then, he had only one goal, and that was to spur the company to action, to execute.

Despite its ailments, Gerstner had a lot of faith in IBM, in its products and its people. No company could have brought in almost $63 billion in annual revenues (as IBM had in 1993) without doing a lot right. He clung to that notion, believing there was nothing inherently wrong with IBM, not with its products, not even with its marketing. Still, something needed repair.

In his view, IBM was simply NOT EXECUTING WELL ENOUGH. It was as if a baseball coach had designed the greatest strategies, put the best players on the field, but then neglected to give the team an adequate amount of time to learn and practice the plays. When he made the rounds of IBM very early in the job, Lou Gerstner was upset at what he found: all kinds of perfectly good product and marketing plans that had not left the tops of executives' desks. Constantly he inquired how a certain product had done once it got to market, only to learn that the product had never been launched. That meant, plain and simple, it had racked up zero sales. Gerstner was flabbergasted. How could this have happened? No one seemed to know. Or perhaps more

accurately, no one was brave enough to tell him. But Lou
Gerstner knew.

FALLING ASLEEP ON THE JOB

It was the absence of a disciplined organization to blame. People
had fallen asleep on the job. They were simply not doing their
assignments. It wasn't the employees' fault. Gerstner knew who
was to blame: his predecessors. They had allowed this "execution" gap to occur.

He emphasized that IBM had great products, great people, and a
great reputation. What it had lacked in the past was a will to get
the job done. The only issue was the company's ability to execute. IBM needed to get its diverse units to work together. The
sales staff had been so spoiled by years of success and the
bureaucracy had become so bloated, that Big Blue had found it
difficult to respond quickly to change in the marketplace. Rather
than work as a team, IBM employees would rather undercut one
another.

Gerstner needed to teach the company the true meaning of execution. As he often said, execution did not mean simply attending meetings or convening task forces, nor did it mean debating
issues and researching opportunities. Execution meant closing
deals, seeing customers, shipping products, and meeting and
beating targets. It was not how many hours one worked or how
long the meetings lasted. It was working on the right things, the
things with the highest marketplace impact.

From then on, Gerstner made clear, any employee not focusing
on anything but "the right things" would not fare well. Either the
person would learn to execute, or there would be a different kind
of "execution," one that would be career-ending for the
employee. All of this defined Lou Gerstner's discipline.

Some had insisted that IBM should become a services company; that, although it had been the greatest technology business on the planet, it no longer could develop the right products. Gerstner at first rejected such notions, arguing that IBM was the technology leader in the industry. The way to get IBM back on track was not to dispense with its manufacturing side, but to improve the way the company's products got to market. IBM's customers knew that it was the technology leader. The problem was getting the technology to market quickly without major quality issues. Gerstner was determined that IBM would recommit itself to getting high-quality products to market quickly.

EXECUTION—proper execution—was the best way to fix things, Gerstner asserted. In any transformation like the one IBM was making, the hard part was not launching initiatives, it was seeing them through.

What was keeping IBM from executing?

Gerstner began to sense that A SET OF ROADBLOCKS, some obvious, some subtle, had constrained IBM, making it more and more difficult to implement business plans. One constraint was the long-standing no-layoff policy. When the company was doing well, the policy proved of little harm; but in tough times, when IBM's sales were dropping, the company's costs remained large while revenues dropped. When outright dismissals were required, all the pre-Gerstner regime did was implement a series of measures that permitted employees to take generous retirement packages. But such attrition did not affect the bottom line sufficiently. Finally putting an end to IBM's long-standing no-layoff policy, Gerstner announced the actual firing of 35,000 employees during the summer of 1993.

CONSTRUCTIVE IMPATIENCE

To get IBM employees to execute properly, Gerstner felt he had to convey a SENSE OF URGENCY. He felt he had his work cut out for him. He felt that IBM personnel took too long to make decisions. Staffers still talked too much in large committees. They continued to study things too much. Perhaps most important, there was no sense of urgency within the company. Gerstner often said that being fast could be better than being insightful; fast did not mean reckless, it meant moving projects along with a sense that things must get done today, not tomorrow. He urged on every IBM employee a huge dose of what he called constructive impatience.

DISCIPLINE

What's another way of saying constructive impatience? DISCIPLINE!

To bring off the recovery of IBM, Gerstner did not feel he needed any fancy strategies. All he had to do was to get IBM employees to do their jobs better, to execute. That was the only strategy needed.

Eventually, IBM executives began to take Gerstner seriously. Sam Palmisano, who would be chosen to replace Gerstner early in 2002 as the new IBM CEO, was put in charge of the PC division in April 1996, with the hope that he would come up with ways to spur growth. Keeping in mind that Gerstner was harping on execution, Palmisano set an agenda for himself: To attract new customers, half of the products his division produced that year would be new. He was in the job only three weeks when he concluded that this was an impossible goal under existing circumstances. During a visit to the PC manufacturing complex in

Raleigh, NC, he watched the snail's pace and was desperate to speed things up. At 7 a.m. one day, he gathered the manufacturing team together and delivered a short speech that echoed his desperation.

He reassigned senior executives to different responsibilities. Employees were instructed to attend only those meetings that were vital to their work, freeing them to do more product testing, and to accelerate the pace of testing. Palmisano spurred the sales force to start pushing products seriously even before those products were ready for market. A sales rep told him that if they did that and missed the marketing deadline, they would not be considered a reliable supplier. Palmisano replied that if they did not push products now, sales would be lost. Six weeks later, PCs rolled out the door. For the first time in the decade, IBM's PCs were first to market; as a result, the unit gained a full market share point in each of the last three quarters of 1996. Palmisano threw a large year-end celebration and gave his employees bonuses—the first they'd seen in years.

To Gerstner, discipline meant WORKING FAST.

By the end of 1996, Gerstner could see that IBM was finally displaying great improvement in its sense of urgency and execution. He was pleased that the IBM culture was now focusing on speed. Analysts began to notice the difference, too. Frank Dzubeck, President of Communications Network Architects, found IBM personnel working when he called at 6 p.m. They were giving home phone numbers, encouraging people to call them in the evenings and on weekends. E-mails were being returned quickly.

Part of IBM's new disciplined mode of operation was PROMISING ONLY WHAT COULD TRULY BE DELIVERED. Gerstner had learned the value of such a policy before taking over IBM. Overpromising, he knew, was counter-productive, damaging to one's reputation, and ultimately lost customers.

No Over-Promising

Accordingly, he refused to pledge to shareholders that he would turn IBM around immediately. He predicted that a turnover would take possibly five or ten years, though in fact it took him far less time. Not over-promising made him look that much better.

Nothing mattered to Gerstner as much as execution. He believed that if IBM employees did their jobs as well as possible, the company would flourish. The largest challenge at IBM, he liked to say, was execution. IBM was, in his view, the most complex company in the world, not simply because of its size and breadth, but because of its technology. How to get 300,000 employees in 170 countries to execute was his key managerial test.

He knew that if he could shorten the meetings, get his executives to make decisions faster, and get products to market more rapidly, he would be able to move IBM in the right direction.

Pressure built on Gerstner from Wall Street and elsewhere to show quick results, higher short-term revenues. Gerstner preferred building a smooth-running, efficient organization. He might have sought to get all the revenue possible from IBM's businesses at first, and fix only those things that were broken; however, he refused to defer the tough, hard steps needed to turn the company around. He chose to get rid of those businesses that might have given him some short-term revenue, but were largely under-performing. For instance, he dropped IBM's printing business. He was also determined to make IBM's PC division run more smoothly, and so he focused on reducing costs, managing inventory and distribution, and getting products out quickly, before price-cutting. As a result, the division returned to profitability by 1995, after losing as much as $1 billion.

Creating a disciplined organization also meant taking a good hard look at the changing business environment. Gerstner sensed that computer consumers were increasingly interested in companies that supplied the knowledge of how to run computers, and not the computers themselves. He found the computer industry too focused on its hardware: mainframes, networks, software, and PCs. Customers suffered as a result. He wanted to respond to the customers' needs.

He knew that customers did not wake up and say, "Oh boy, I want to go buy a new operating system." They got up and said, "How do I make my bank more successful?"

Through the rigor of DISCIPLINE, he eventually turned the company into A MORE COMPETITIVE PLACE that was more customer-oriented, and more conscious of the changing business environment. He honed IBM into a fighting machine that could ruthlessly execute.

STRESSING THE SERVICES SIDE

Gerstner built up a very strong services business, which was a major factor in the resurgence of IBM. He explained that the computer services that helped corporations manage their operations would eventually surpass hardware as a company's biggest business. By 1996, IBM's services business had surpassed software for the first time to become the company's second-largest revenue producer. Still, that was less than half of hardware sales.

Gerstner moved quickly and came in with some incredible results almost immediately. A year after taking office, he announced that he was reasonably comfortable that the worst was behind him, that IBM had stabilized. It had come out of the restructuring period. Most people agreed, giving him high first-year marks for cutting costs, building up IBM's cash reserves, and restoring profitability. In January 1994, Big Blue reported a profit for fourth-quarter 1993, its first profit in six quarters. In April of that year, just in time for its annual shareholders meeting in Toronto, IBM, shocking Wall Street, announced first-quarter net income of $392 million—over five times what most analysts had expected.

How had Gerstner produced these profits?

His heavy cost-cutting efforts, for one thing. Annual expenses for sales, administration, research, and other matters not directly tied to products dropped to $24 billion from $27 billion, then to $17 billion a year. He also slashed the IBM annual dividend twice his first year at the helm, reducing the quarterly payout to 25 cents a share from $1.21 a share in 1992.

A Desk Is a Dangerous Place

To set an example as "MR. DISCIPLINARIAN," Gerstner logged over 150,000 air miles during his first year as he met customers and employees around the world. He visited all large IBM customers and many small ones. He summoned staff to meetings, asking them for their views of how to fix the company. He understood that to get the job done, he had to get away from corporate headquarters. Above his desk was a quote from spy novelist John Le Carre: "A desk is a dangerous place from which to watch the world."

Gerstner conveyed a no-nonsense message. He cut meetings short and expressed annoyance at anyone who wasted time. He outlawed the so-called foils, or prepared slides and overhead projector presentations that were used regularly pre-Gerstner to bolster a position or decision. In the past, IBM's executives would spend days making these foils for meetings.

He told employees at IBM Research, a pure research laboratory, that it could no longer operate as if it were on the dole. It had to cut costs and get more aggressive about patents; it had to make the business of licensing technology lucrative. Eventually, under Gerstner, it did all that, winning more patents than any other company each year.

He worried a good deal about IBM becoming complacent again. In August 1994, he fired off a memo via e-mail warning his employees not to begin the celebrations just because the company seemed to be turned around. He sensed that there was a temptation to sit back and start humming *Happy Days Are Here Again,* to feel that things were back to normal once again and it would be possible to return to the old IBM. But those days were gone forever, he insisted.

The industry was changing too rapidly to warrant such complacency. Competition was too tough. Profit margins were too weak. IBM's costs remained higher than its rivals', and its culture was way too bureaucratic. He noted that IBM employees were still too preoccupied with process, meetings, and bureaucracy. He pointed to bureaucratic infighting, a problem that was still hurting the company. He urged everyone not to focus on the opponents down the hall. Instead, they should concentrate on competitors. You could be sure, he said, that they have been focused on IBM for years.

He cited employees who sent him e-mail expressing frustration over the IBM bureaucracy. He too got frustrated, but he would make sure that IBM made the changes it had to make. He would make sure to re-energize IBM. He thanked everyone at IBM who had supported change and warned those who had not that the train was leaving the station. It was time to hop aboard or be left behind.

Example after example of "The Disciplinarian" at work exists: One day while on the job very early, Gerstner sought to move a product announcement up a few days to beat a competitor to market. Employees informed him that he could not do what he wanted because IBM only unveiled products the first and third Tuesdays of the month. Guess what? Lou got the date changed. If he didn't like a part of the IBM culture, he just changed it.

On one of his first days at the company, Gerstner arrived wearing a blue shirt; in a previous era, this was practically an act of betrayal in the land of starched white shirts. Though he had not been trying to communicate a new message to the staff, Gerstner created a blue-shirt culture within three months. By then he was sending a message: I don't care what the color of your shirt is as long as you get results.

In executing the resurgence, Gerstner re-established IBM as the world's foremost computer company. By 1996, he had slashed IBM's costs by $7 billion. He reversed the trend during which IBM lost money for three straight years: 1991, 1992, and 1993. Since Gerstner had taken over, IBM's stock price had increased about 700%, and its market value grew by $180 billion. It was now one of the three main players in business computing, competing against Sun Microsystems and Microsoft.

Upon his retirement, he sent an e-mail to IBM employees; in it Gerstner observed that all the hard work had returned IBM to its place in the sun. Its strategies were now correct; no one could rival its capacity to innovate. Its culture was moving in the right direction. And, everyone now felt renewed pride in the company. Back in 1993, those had been remote targets. Many had written IBM off; many thought IBM did not have the will to survive, but survive it had, thanks to the disciplinarian.

In the next chapter, we will look at a business leader who focused on the notion of alignment. By introducing alignment into all phases of his business, he was able to bring his company back from the brink.

7

THE IMPORTANCE OF CONSISTENCY: HARRY KRAEMER ALIGNING THE NEW BAXTER

Since being selected as CEO of Baxter International, the global medical-products company, in 1999, Harry Kraemer has transformed the company into one of the industry's most successful and consistent growth engines. Revenue and operating profit have outpaced major indices over the past five years, with stockholder return surpassing both the S&P 500 and S&P Healthcare Composite. Although, 2002 brought unprecedented levels of economic, political, and competitive volatility, Baxter still delivered 10 percent sales growth for the year. In contrast, the median growth in revenues for Fortune 500 companies was just 1.2 percent in 2002.

Throughout his tenure at Baxter, Kraemer has always placed a heavy emphasis on consistency, balance, and alignment, all of which continue to serve a critical role in the company's success.

The company's success can be in large measure due to Kraemer's zealous pursuit of a concept that is called ALIGNMENT. As noted earlier, alignment is basically same-page thinking and represents all those efforts by which a business leader makes sure that all parts of the company are working in harmony.

Baxter's unique combination of expertise in medical devices, pharmaceuticals, and biotechnology enables the development of innovative therapies that provide a tremendous competitive advantage. Baxter is a leading healthcare company involved in providing critical therapies to patients around the world with life-threatening conditions. It started in the field of sterile intravenous fluids more than 70 years ago, and that expertise has evolved into areas including intravenous fluids and pumps; anesthesia products; plasma-based and recombinant therapeutic proteins; products for patients with kidney disease; vaccines; and systems used in the collection, storage, and separation of blood and blood components. Today, the company's products and services are used to treat patients with many conditions including cancer, trauma, hemophilia, immune deficiencies, infectious diseases, kidney disease, and other disorders. Baxter has more than 55,000 team members located in more than 100 countries.

Baxter went public on May 1, 1961. Over time, the company became involved in other activities, including distribution, cardiovascular equipment, and diagnostics. But under Kraemer's leadership, over the last decade many of those businesses were either divested or spun off very successfully as separate, stand-alone, publicly traded companies.

By investing heavily in manufacturing facilities and important technology platforms in recent years, Baxter has gained a great deal of specialized capacity which allows it to produce genetically engineered vaccines and blood-clotting products—two of its most promising businesses.

Harry Kraemer became Baxter's chief executive officer in January 1999 and chairman of Baxter's board of directors in January 2000. He originally joined Baxter in 1982 as director of corporate development. Before joining Baxter, Kraemer worked for Bank of America in corporate banking and for Northwest Industries in planning and business development. His career at Baxter has included senior positions in both domestic and international operations. In 1993, he was named senior vice president and CFO, responsible for all financial operations, business development, communications, and European operations. Over the next several years, he assumed additional responsibility for the company's renal, medication delivery, Japan, and fenwal (now known as transfusion therapies) businesses. In April 1997, he was named president of Baxter International Inc.

At the time he became senior vice president and CFO in 1993, Baxter had lost its focus, and its stock was floundering. It had hit the wall. By the early 1990s, the company had grown out of balance as Baxter sought greater growth and took more risks. But, as so often happens, an over-focus on growth—which Baxter experienced in the early 1990s—meant less thought was given to operational excellence (performance). Kraemer explained, "The tendency to go off the track is very high because any tendency to provide a certain amount of discipline and guard rails go out the window—the rationale being that those things hinder growth." For nine years (1984–1993), aiming for growth, the company encountered a number of challenges, reflected in a diminishing stock price.

In 1993, Baxter's senior leadership, Kraemer included, decided that it made more sense to SEEK A STRONG LEVEL OF OPERATIONAL EXCELLENCE OVER A LONG-TERM GROWTH PROFLE . It was during that year that Kraemer rose to become a senior vice president and CFO. He led the company's efforts to simplify its business practices and to get down to basics. A decision was made: "We really had to get our operational act together."

Getting that act together meant in large measure putting the brakes on the wrong kind of growth. Baxter's leaders brushed aside all talk of growth that was not profitable, sustainable, or capital efficient. Indeed, at the time, Baxter owned several businesses where the faster they grew, the more money they lost. In a few situations, Baxter had businesses where the cost of running them outweighed the overall benefits. Over the next several years, Baxter took important steps to focus on three core businesses: bioscience, medication delivery, and renal. As part of these efforts, the company divested its laboratory and scientific equipment business in, and eventually spun off Allegiance Corporation (which was subsequently acquired by Cardinal Health).

Growth could remain a company goal—not the only goal by any means—but it would have to meet certain defined criteria. It had to be PROFTABLE, SUSTAINABLE, and CAPITAL EFFCIENT . The thinking back then, recalled Kraemer, was: "If it's not profitable, sustainable, and capital efficient, let's not even talk about being desirous of growth."

More than anything else, Kraemer believed that a company's strength lay in setting and meeting its financial commitments—and being consistent in communicating what those financial commitments should and would be.

SEEKING ALIGNMENT

As the company stock took a nosedive during a nine-year period, it occurred to Kraemer and other Baxter executives that the problem came down to alignment.

There was simply not an ALIGNMENT OF EXPECTATIONS between Baxter and, in this case, its shareholders. It occurred to Kraemer that he and his fellow senior executives would have to do a better job of setting those expectations: "If you really have your act together and you're really disciplined, you're really focused, you will set the expectations and have the ability to deliver those results."

DON'T FIXATE ON EXPECTATIONS

Far too often, Kraemer insisted, executives become fixated with the question: ARE WE MEETING EXPECTATIONS? That suggests a certain powerlessness and leads to frantic worries about why the company lost immense stock value after missing expectations by a single penny.

Because Baxter had not been terribly consistent with meeting those expectations prior to 1993, it suffered a credibility gap. And so a light went on for Kraemer: He knew that they had to be certain they were setting very clear expectations, that they would meet every expectation that was set, and that they must explain to people everything they were doing and why simultaneously.

In short, there had to be alignment between the Baxter management team and Wall Street. It began with Kraemer, still the CFO, emphasizing with the Baxter management team that "we're not the victim here." He firmly believed that if the company set realistic expectations, communicated those expectations clearly, and delivered against them, it could have a good deal of influence. Indeed, if Wall Street analysts believed that Baxter would beat expectations, it meant they'd done a really, really poor job of communicating what they were going to do. To Kraemer, Baxter executives could not permit Wall Street analysts to put pressure on the company by getting ahead of Baxter. In other words, he wanted Baxter to set the Street's expectations, not the other way around.

From the period of 1993 through mid-2002, Baxter hit its sales and earnings targets every quarter and doubled its goal for annual growth in income, to a growth rate of 15 percent.

ALL ABOARD!

While messages went out externally to PRESERVE ALIGNMENT WITH WALL STREET, Kraemer was busy working on alignment within the management team, an equally important pursuit.

At the same time, Kraemer understood that in order to improve the business he had to get all of its various parts working in order. He saw the necessity of getting his senior executives to align themselves with various elements of the company.

PROVIDING INCENTIVES TO EXECUTIVES TO MAKE SURE THEY DID THEIR JOBS AS THEY SHOULD AND TO MAKE SURE THEY ALIGNED THEMSELVES WITH THOSE ASPECTS OF THE COMPANY THAT COUNTED, KRAEMER BUILT A NEW CULTURE AT BAXTER BASED ON PERFORMANCE AND ACCOUNTABILITY.

Baxter has been recognized over the last several years for its innovative executive compensation programs that provide incentives to senior management to drive shareholder value. For example, Baxter was one of the first companies, more than a decade ago, to compensate its board of directors with stock options as a way to more align them with driving value for shareholders.

"Shareholders invest in a company with the expectation that they will see gains in the form of an increased stock price, as well as through dividends," Kraemer commented.

Baxter's employee compensation programs were structured to reward the desired employee performance and hold them accountable for delivering the targeted performance. Clearly, one of the performance parameters was to drive increased shareholder value. There are a number of ways to align employee compensation with shareholder interests, including stock options, and stock grants.

That was exactly why Kraemer established the company's first Shared Investment Plan (SIP) in 1994 and a second plan in 1999. Under the SIP, participants took out personal, full-recourse loans at considerable personal financial risk to purchase at market price, large numbers of shares of Baxter stock. Specifically under the 1999 SIP, 142 of Baxter's senior managers used five-year, full-recourse, market-rate personal bank loans to purchase 6.2 million shares of Baxter stock for cash at the May 3, 1999, closing price of $31.81 (adjusted for stock split in 2001, but not adjusted for the spin-off of Edwards Lifesciences in 2000).

Kraemer strongly believed that the SIP program was in the best long-term interests of all of shareholders because it so closely linked senior managers' personal financial interests with those of shareholders. As a team, they would continue to look for ways to structure compensation and incentives in a manner that would drive value for their shareholders.

Kraemer also noted that this alignment in compensation helped break down silos between businesses and encouraged managers to make decisions based on what was right for shareholders and Baxter overall, and not necessarily on what was in the best interests of a particular business. He hammered home to senior executives that they must decide on capital expenditures for their own business units based on what was good for the company overall—and not just narrowly what was good for their own units. He gave the example of one business unit leader seeking $50 million in capital expenditure for his own unit.

He did not want another business unit leader keeping silent rather feeling free to speak out against the $50 million proposal. He wanted his colleagues to feel free to challenge fellow executives. He did not want anyone to say: "I've got enough problems so I'm not going to challenge the $50 million proposal. I'll let the CEO and the CFO do that. And by the way, I'm not going to rain on the proposal because I might be looking for $50 million in capital expenditures next month."

According to Harry Kraemer, such thinking was "old world."

STRATEGIC BYWORDS

For Kraemer, part of being consistent, part of doing what you say all the time, is adhering to some fairly simple strategic bywords: They are:

- Focus

- Discipline

- Credibility

- Communication

It is this mantra that Kraemer repeated over and over again: "If we're focused, and we're disciplined, and we're consistent, we can have an enormous impact on the stock price."

KRAEMER BELIEVES THAT EVERYTHING COMES DOWN TO COMMUNICATION. He answers about 120 voice mails a day. He returns all calls in a day. He can e-mail 20,000 people at once. Each Monday, Kraemer meets with his team to deal with the "stuck" issues. To him, no problem should take longer than 168 hours (a week). He keeps all 55,000 employees (in 103 countries) on the same page by making sure that everyone understands what Baxter is trying to do, and what the employee role is. Each month, Kraemer writes a lengthy note. In it, he talks about strategy and goals. The letter, which he started in 1992 as CFO, went to 150 managers at first. By the end of 2001, it was going to 25,000 plus. Kraemer includes humor and colorful stories.

To Kraemer, it really comes down to a few simple questions: Are you a leader who can balance self-confidence and humility? Are you encouraging people to challenge you as opposed to surrounding yourself with yes people? Are the people who push against you the strongest? Are you keeping things unbelievably simple? Are you communicating your brains out?

Simplicity also shines through in the strategic outlook for Baxter.

With everyone moving so quickly, Kraemer thinks you need to keep it real simple.

He does this by communicating consistently and clearly—using FOUR KEY TERMS—Best Team, Best Partner, Best Investment, and Best Citizen—to describe the company's strategies, insisting that the company be consistent to its employees and to Wall Street, and demanding that the company deliver on its commitments.

Kraemer's disciplined strategy toward acquisitions also has increased the company's numbers. He will only purchase another firm if he believes that it will generate an after-tax rate of return of at least 20 percent. In June 2002, Baxter finalized its fifth acquisition in 16 months.

While sticking to the basics, Kraemer believes as well that the company has to be MANAGED FOR THE LONG TERM.

SHORT TERM AND LONG TERM

Kraemer doesn't think a company can survive if it doesn't maintain a view both to the sky and on the ground. To him, if you're not watching what's happening around and above you, you're managing with your head down, and you're setting yourself up for serious trouble. "Somebody who says, 'I'm going to focus on meeting my commitment this year, the hell with next year, I'll worry about that next year' clearly is not balancing the short and long term."

Managing short term is critical (in this case, being consistent and meeting Wall Street's expectations each quarter) because to do otherwise—to miss the numbers—creates uncertainty about how well the company can predict what it will do in the long term.

Managing long term is equally critical, Kraemer insists. He gives the example of Baxter in 2001: It ended up making $1.75 per share, even as it increased research and development costs by 14 percent and capital expenditures by 25 percent. But some Baxter executives, fearing that it would be hard to reach $1.75 a share, could have urged slowing down on R&D expenditures. Kraemer suggests that taking such a view would have been harmful in the long term. What would have happened, he asked hypothetically, if instead of earning $1.75 a share, Baxter earned $1.80, but R&D declined by 5 percent (rather than increasing by 15 percent)?

Kraemer argues that the stock might not have risen but declined because the perception would have been that Baxter was not preparing itself (through increased R&D spending) for the long term.

Kraemer's zealous commitment to aligning the company with Wall Street analysts and shareholders, fellow executives, and employees, and his insistence on reaching a balance between short-term and long-term initiatives has led to some very healthy returns. In the period of 1999–2002, Baxter has outperformed its peers, with compounded annual growth in EPS of 13.7 percent, and revenue growth of 9.2 percent. In 1994, Baxter had an 11 percent operating margin, a $20 stock price, a 10 P/E multiple, and market cap of $4 billion. Eight years later, in 2002, it was at the equivalent of $122 (including the impact of stock dividends from the spinoffs and a stock split); it had a P/E multiple of 32, and a market cap of $32 billion.

Like many other companies, Baxter has faced a significant decline in the stock's performance in late 2002 and early 2003 as a result of the unprecedented market and political volatility that has occurred. But through it all, Kraemer attributes the company's continued solid performance to employees who understand the importance of both balancing both the short term and long term, and driving the short-term performance. This is because they now know to never lose sight of their four strategic bywords: Focus, Discipline, Credibility, and Communication. He also believes that alignment isn't a one-time event or something to revisit only when hitting the wall. It's a continuous process.

As Kraemer likes to say, "You've got this incredible calibration. Balancing growth and performance comes down to alignment— an alignment between short-term and long-term business decisions." For example, what is the highest short-term performance your company can achieve that allows for the optimal long-term results? Perhaps you could deliver 20 percent earnings growth this year, but if you instead achieved 10 and invested the balance in your product pipeline, production facilities, you could achieve much more three or four years from now. What's the highest short term that optimizes the future? That's the critical question for Kraemer.

The next part will deal with the last of the three strategies in which executives have to perform well to set their companies right again: critical capabilities.

BREAKING THROUGH THE WALL

8

CRITICAL CAPABILITIES: ACTIONS THAT MAKE A DIFFERENCE

THE RUTHLESS EXECUTION CHECKLIST

1. Do you have a cost and working capital management program that is driven throughout the business?

2. Do you have a proactive and disciplined approach to identifying and assessing potential acquisitions and divestitures?

3. Do you regularly assess whether the corporate center is adding distinctive value to each business unit?

4. Do you effectively and swiftly manage out non-performers?

It has been asserted throughout this book that if executives are to overcome business setbacks, they must demonstrate an ability to consistently execute in the following three strategies:

■ LEADERSHIP

■ GOVERNANCE

■ CRITICAL CAPABILITIES

This chapter looks at the third element that executives need to overcome business reversals: CRITICAL CAPABILITIES, OR THE SPECIFC ACTIONS THAT EXECUTIVES DRIVE TO BREAK THROUGH THE WALL.

CAPABILITIES ARE NOT COMPETENCIES

Very much at the core or heart of what a company does, competencies are the ways that the company differentiates itself. For some companies, like Cisco Systems, for example, a competency can be its sales force or its acquisition and integration capabilities; for another company, like GE, it might be its uncanny ability to create synergies among its businesses.

CRITICAL CAPABILITIES, on the other hand, are the recalibrating actions that need to become part of the corporate fabric. They are the essential triggers or springboards required for improved performance.

The same point made in the earlier leadership and governance segments holds true for critical capabilities: Leaders who have successfully broken through the wall all have had certain critical capabilities that were very visible in common.

These critical capabilities include:

1. VIGILANT PRODUCTIVITY MANAGEMENT

2. CRITICAL TALENT MANAGEMENT

3. FOCUSED CORPORATE TRANSACTIONS

VIGILANT PRODUCTIVITY MANAGEMENT

Included in this critical capability are cost management, working capital management, and technology-driven productivity improvement. Companies that have been able to overcome previous business reversals have these critical capabilities in common.

COST MANAGEMENT

Companies that have broken through the wall had to be discriminating regarding cost management. They almost never cut to the bone, and more important, they never took such measures across-the-board. Although their vigilance around operational excellence focused on improving both general and administrative expenses (G&A) and cost of goods sold (COGS), they focused most of their attention on year-over-year operations improvements (COGS, working capital). That focus was a key differentiator among these business leaders and their companies.

Why does traditional cost management fail? Broad cost reduction efforts—promoted with slogans such as "Reduce costs by 10 percent"—often fail because they do not recognize the differences in customer value and behavior. Often, a small segment of customers account for the majority of customer value or profitability for a company. Thus, an across-the-board cut is like shooting oneself in the foot.

Successful leaders make sure that they connect their cost drivers to how their businesses create value. This is not a trivial exercise. Most companies either don't have the talent required to do this, or are not willing to invest the time, and most always opt instead for a quick fix. Successful leaders also reduce their working capital; renegotiate debt and take advantage of cheaper financing and cheaper growth opportunities (e.g., acquisitions); and finally, they critically re-calibrate their capital investments and get rid of non-performing investments.

THE NEVER-ENDING STORY

Simply cutting the budget does not work. Companies are not improving cost efficiencies by reducing the budget and taking out headcount. They will find that the headcount removed quickly comes back to them in spades, especially if times get better. Productivity and efficiency must be part of the equation.

It is crucial to define the cost targets and expected operating environment in which a business finds itself. Executives must understand their own company's customer base and how profit and value are allocated within that base. It's then possible to look at what products and services most attract customer value and how effective the company is in delivering them, and to look at what percentage of the company's resources are devoted to customer segments of marginal appeal. That percentage must be reduced by some means. Business leaders have to look at what non-strategic services should be outsourced to more efficient providers, and they must decide what customer segments or channel areas should be given up completely.

WORKING CAPITAL MANAGEMENT

Improving working capital should be a key area of focus for corporate leaders. Fundamentally, managing working capital is a way to increase returns to the company. It allows leaders to increase the cash flow used for investment. Opportunities for working capital improvement differ across industries, but they typically involve a focus on key business processes such as inventory, accounts payable, and receivables. For example, because Dell holds inventory for such short periods of time versus its peer group, it has negative working capital and has actually decreased its need for capital as the company has grown significantly.

In industries that are capital and asset intensive (discrete manufacturing, retail), return on assets (RONA) and return on capital employed (ROCE) are measures that get significant leadership attention. However, it is often the case that the dollars tied up in working capital get ignored. This working capital can often make up to more than 15 percent of the total capital. Part of the problem is that working capital is very much tied into many other parts of the company where accountability is divided across different organizations and the key drivers to working capital efficiency are often hidden in subprocesses, making it difficult to see at the senior executive level.

Effectively managing working capital can make the difference between success and failure, especially in economic slowdowns and anemic earnings periods. The trick is understanding the key drivers that influence working capital the most in each organization and effectively motivating business leaders to manage those things they can control (not an easy task).

DELL'S DRIVE FOR CASH

In 1993, Dell was facing a serious liquidity problem. Their rapid growth coupled with poor working capital management, was rapidly constraining their ability to grow in the future. To remedy the problem, Dell institutionalized a working capital program that clearly incentivized the different decision makers to have a keen focus on cash flow and a more efficient cash management process. Today, working capital management is part of the Dell fabric.

More important, these leaders don't view cost and working capital management as a one-time event. Rather, it is a part of the corporate DNA of these business leaders, and ultimately their companies. Because of this, these leaders can sustain their cost performance significantly longer than their rivals. Others typically find themselves cutting costs as a reaction to a bad situation. This is often too little, too late.

TECHNOLOGY-DRIVEN PRODUCTIVITY IMPROVEMENT

Another characteristic of leaders who have broken through the wall is that they were smart about information technology (IT). They managed their IT investments better than their less-successful peer group. They devoted significant attention to technology investments, getting more involved in the planning, execution, and review of their investments. They had a keen, singleminded focus on using IT to drive process and productivity improvement.

IT-smart companies see returns from their technology investments that are superior to their rivals (see Figure 8–1):

- They optimize existing processes for incremental productivity improvements, resulting in 10–15 percent G&A savings.

- They reconstruct core processes for changes in productivity and efficiency, resulting in 2–3 percent operating margin improvements.

- In a few cases, they invent new processes and organizational capabilities for growth that can result in ten-fold return on invested capital (ROIC).

Leaders who were less successful with their recovery efforts had difficulty calculating how much they actually spend on technology, and how to prioritize their tech spending. They often found themselves viewing IT as strategic early in the fiscal year, and a cost by year's end.

Most companies cannot measure the ROI that IT generates. Research indicates that these companies are barely covering their cost of capital.

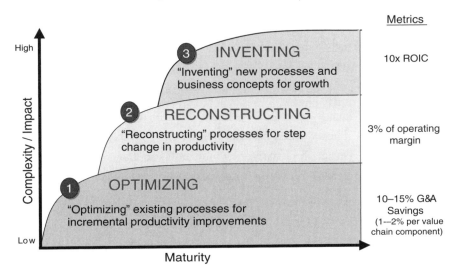

FIGURE 8–1
Companies that ruthlessly execute realize benefits driven by a focus on productivity and process improvement.

The successful leaders I studied were very focused with their technology efforts and often spent less on IT than their peers. However, they approached technology with certain principles in mind:

- **PRINCIPLE 1**: Make IT a business-driven activity (i.e., optimize IT as an asset).

- **PRINCIPLE 2**: Ensure IT is focused on doing the right things, instead of doing things right.

- **PRINCIPLE 3**: Be unrelenting about IT's link to the business strategy.

- **PRINCIPLE 4**: Ensure rigor in IT prioritization, investment, and measurement.

- **PRINCIPLE 5**: Avoid over-commitment to IT initiatives.

- **PRINCIPLE 6**: Demand measurable milestones in three-month increments.

TALENT MANAGEMENT

Talent management is fundamentally about putting the right people in the right places, and keeping them over the long haul.

The business leaders I studied clearly understood their talent pool. They worked hard to identify the key players who had critical relationships with customers and suppliers, and then worked even harder to nurture and keep those players.

A number of business leaders have asserted that coming up with the best talent for their companies is the most important task they have to perform. Some, like Jack Welch and Honeywell International's Larry Bossidy, spent an inordinate amount of time searching for the best talent within their own employee pools, hoping to build leadership that way. Both Welch and Bossidy have said frequently that all the great strategies in the world will have little effect on a company unless THE RIGHT PEOPLE ARE CHOSEN TO EXECUTE THOSE STRATEGIES.

The leaders I studied understood this and put a premium on keeping the talent they needed for growth. They did what it took to ensure that key people were secure and did not leave because of low morale, thus preventing a defection domino effect.

WINNER TAKES ALL

The most important thing a business leader can do to attract and keep top talent is to TURN IN A WINNING PERFORMANCE YEAR AFTER YEAR. It's nice and important to be part of a great place to work with great benefits. But, top talent wants to be with a winner and a company that is going places.

Part of this critical capability is the awareness of keeping only the best performers, getting rid of the bottom 10 percent of people who are not performing up to standard, and going through this weeding-out process on a regular basis (yearly) and by doing so, upgrade the talent and performance pool.

COME OUT, COME OUT, WHEREVER YOU ARE

How long does your company carry non-performers? In most large organizations, you would be surprised at the amount of time one can survive without performing. This includes senior management. Whether it is due to bureaucracy or some other reason, it takes too long. Anything longer than 12 months should not be tolerated.

Significantly, just as with the effort to keep costs and working capital managed and under control, the leaders who figured out how to break through the wall did not treat talent management as a one-time event, something to look at once a year and then move on to more important areas of the company. They took talent management so seriously that they were systematically and strategically searching through and outside their company on a regular basis for the right talent to promote. That explains why companies that successfully broke through the wall routinely spread their recruitment nets first and foremost within their own employee ranks but in the end would go to great lengths to bring in top talent wherever they found it.

Searching within one's ranks is, however, a more difficult task than hiring an outside recruiter or search firm to fill an external requisition. It requires great energy and an established process of identification and cultivation on the part of management or human resources to produce potential leaders from within one's own employee population. Cisco Systems found this out the hard way: After it had suffered a huge business setback in the winter of 2001, the company's human resources executives began a fresh effort to take a close look at its employees to find out who had the most potential for leadership roles within the company. This form of talent management had been a luxury when the company was doing well; but in bad times, Cisco's executives felt that it was crucial to deal very carefully with those employees who could move up the ranks.

Wal-Mart has been making new efforts to train leadership within its ranks as well. Selected employees are asked to attend leadership training sessions with top executives on various topics, all with the idea of helping those employees take on more responsible roles within the company.

BRINGING ON THE BEST

What do business leaders look for in hiring high-quality employees? AOL Time Warner's Steve Case, when he was running AOL, looked for passion. He liked to say that people were going to make mistakes—especially if they were passionate—but their energy and commitment eventually made them winners. AT&T's Michael Armstrong wanted new hires to be willing to take risks and to correct the mistakes they inevitably made.

Cisco Systems' John Chambers assumes that anyone who actually wants to work at his company is less desirable than someone who does not. So, he and his human resources team give preference to the "passive" job seeker, anyone who has not expressed any interest in working for Cisco. Often, Chambers has found, they are better qualified than the aggressive job seeker. Southwest Airlines' Herb Kelleher also takes a counterintuitive approach: If he has a choice between someone who has more experience, more education, or more expertise, and someone who has the right attitude, he'll give preference to the latter. He simply doesn't want to have people around who have what he calls "a lousy attitude." After all, he notes, attitude is the one thing you can't change. Skills you can always teach later.

When each of these business leaders hones in on what kind of person to hire—whether it's the passive job seeker or the one with the best attitude—they are engaging in what is called a RECALIBRATION OF TALENT. That strategy, when pursued properly, inevitably helps these leaders get past their current business difficulties.

No one was defter, or spent more time at, picking the right talent than GE's Jack Welch. He repeatedly asserted that the most important part of his job was to hire the best people, and then let them get on with their work. If he didn't get the people part of his job right, he observed, it was unlikely he would get the strategic business plan part right. So, he spent a good part of each year searching within GE itself for the best talent; then, when he found that talent, he nurtured them, gave them incentives, trained them, and promoted them. Welch's recalibration of talent followed a similar pattern year in and year out.

In April of each year, he attended GE's annual review of the intellectual capital of the company. Welch began attending these annual "Session C" meetings, which ran intermittently for 20 days or so in the spring. A session for a particular business unit took place over one day. GECS, because it was so large, took two days. No one remembers why these meetings were called "Session C."

The "Session C" process actually began in February when every GE employee filled out a self-assessment review. He or she then discussed that review with a manager, and the manager sent an assessment up the management chain.

Welch, along with his vice chairmen and senior human resources personnel, met with each business leader at their respective headquarters.

They also met with senior human resources people at the business. All of the approximately 3,000 people who were in the executive band and above were reviewed at these sessions.

Salaries did not come up for discussion. Instead, Welch and his associates asked: Who is retiring? Who do you want to promote? Who should attend executive classes at Crotonville (GE's leadership institute)?

No single place at GE illustrates the recalibrating of talent as well as the Crotonville Leadership Center, often called the "Harvard of Corporate America." Jack Welch loved the place. It became in Welch's time a chief catalyst for transmitting his business philosophy. But, it was also a cauldron of GE talent, where young executives and managers were given an early opportunity to shine—

or not shine—in front of the people who controlled their trajectory in the company.

Crotonville is located in the Hudson Valley of New York and rests on a 50-acre campus that resembles in many ways a small college. The first major corporate business school, built in 1956, it has a unique flavor to it. While other businesses routinely invite senior executives to seminars or retreats, GE was the first to provide junior executives with extensive coursework and exposure to the brass over more than just a few hours or even a few days.

Courses are taught at Crotonville to upwards of 5,000 GE staffers each year, but rather than the old-style education, where teachers teach and students do little more than listen, GE "students" are encouraged to challenge their "teachers," to question what they are doing, to offer fresh ways of looking at business issues. By watching the give and take, Welch and his human resources team could judge how best to recalibrate talent.

FOCUSED CORPORATE TRANSACTIONS

One of the overriding differences between leaders who have broken through the wall and those who haven't is a keen focus and intensity on mergers, acquisitions, and divestitures.

Business leaders who understand what it takes to get past reversals tend to actively manage their portfolios of business; this is a common characteristic of companies that manage through uncertain times and break through the wall. These leaders must excel not only at managing portfolios, but at managing uncertainties.

If companies are going to recalibrate, one of the best ways to do it is to employ this critical capability, institutionalizing a strategy of searching for mergers, acquisitions, and divestitures.

Here, the term "divestiture" means selling off, not necessarily only a business, but some asset within the business; it could be a functional area of the company such as IT, for example. In other words, outsourcing is very much a part of divestiture.

Unfortunately, the reality of outsourcing is that close to half of all outsourcing efforts fail within five years; so, going the outsourcing route is not easy. Moreover, outsourcing is not necessarily cheaper than performing a function in-house. While companies routinely believe that outsourcing will somehow magically infuse them with cash while lowering costs, world-class in-house capabilities can actually be 20 percent cheaper than if done via outsourcing. Finally, one of the sins that companies often make is they act as if they can outsource accountability when that capability is in someone else's hands. When a company enters into outsourcing, it will still need to devote time, energy, and resources to managing that process to ensure it is delivering value. See Figure 8–2.

AN ACQUISITIVE LOT

Consistent acquisitions and strategic divestitures, in good times and bad, are the hallmark of revitalization.

Acquisitions, of course, are a mainstay of many companies and form the backbone for the growth of numerous enterprises. In fact, a recent Bain & Company[*] study found that companies that acquire often and consistently outperform their peers. For the leaders I studied, top-line growth was a key driver for these deals, as seldom do cost synergies pay for an acquisition. However, these leaders did not allow acquisitions to become the only vehicle for their companies' growth. They would not allow their companies to depend purely on acquisitions for revenue

---

[*].   S. Rovit and C. Lemire, *Harvard Business Review*, (March 2003).

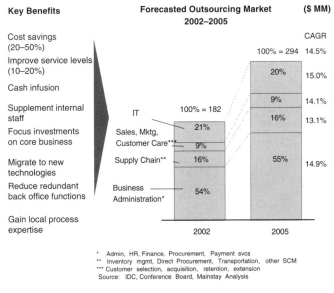

Key Benefits

Cost savings
(20–50%)
Improve service levels
(10–20%)

Cash infusion

Supplement internal
staff
Focus investments
on core business

Migrate to new
technologies
Reduce redundant
back office functions

Gain local process
expertise

Forecasted Outsourcing Market
2002–2005

($ MM)

CAGR
100% = 294 14.5%
20%   15.0%
9%   14.1%
16%   13.1%
55%   14.9%

100% = 182
IT
21%
Sales, Mktg,
Customer Care*** 9%
Supply Chain** 16%
Business
Administration* 54%

2002   2005

*   Admin, HR, Finance, Procurement, Payment svcs
** Inventory mgmt, Direct Procurement, Transportation, other SCM
*** Customer selection, acquisition, retention, extension
Source: IDC, Conference Board, Mainstay Analysis

FIGURE 8–2
Outsourcing.

improvements. These leaders understood that it was imperative to encourage their own products—producing departments to churn out new products—and not rely on an acquired company to fulfill that role. And so, these companies focused on stabilizing and growing their core revenue base as opposed to solely relying on acquisitions as a means to grow. A company that had a problem growing organically would only mask, and perhaps even worsen, its problems by relying on acquisitions.

CHANGING A TIRE WHILE DRIVING THE CAR

A key focus of effective integration is making sure the company doesn't take productivity and revenue hits during the integration process. This is by no means easy to do.

Most companies are better at the deal than they are at integrating an acquired company. Business leaders who have been able to break through the wall have understood that it is more important to focus on the execution and implementation of the acquisition than on the actual acquisition deal itself. Of course, these leaders spent a good deal of time looking over potential companies to purchase. But, they invested huge chunks of time and energy as well in making sure that the acquired company was integrated into the overall company. They tried to understand what the acquired company needed from them in order to make it successful.

Acquired companies need different things from their acquirers. In some cases, if an acquired company is young and in a new growth market, it needs a focus on new product development, new businesses, and forging new alliances; if it's a mature company, it will need help with cost management capabilities and consolidation. Understanding the needs of any company to be acquired and delivering on those needs are strategic necessities.

Business leaders I studied also reviewed post-merger integration efforts for lessons learned. They took great pains to study how the integration of each acquisition went with a view toward making improvements in future acquisitions. It was hard work, and only a few got it.

An Aggressive Acquirer

One CEO who used acquisitions aggressively and with much sophistication was Cisco Systems' John Chambers. Throughout the 1990s, he turned to acquisitions as a critical capability of his company in his quest to grow the business and enter new markets. Until Chambers came along, high-tech companies in Silicon Valley had eschewed such behavior, as the personnel at those enterprises firmly believed that only products that were homegrown had any value. Chambers was an outsider—he came from West Virginia—so it was much easier for him to break with Silicon Valley tradition.

So adept did Chambers become in acquisitions that numerous companies, many of them small start-ups, practically begged him to take them over. But Chambers did not believe that every acquisition would work. He knew that, in general, acquisitions were difficult to do, and integrating the parent and newly acquired company was especially hard.

Sometimes, acquisitions did not work because the cultures of the two companies clashed or the timing of an acquisition was poor (e.g., Cisco might have acquired a business that had yet to produce marketable products.) Still, at least according to Chambers, Cisco Systems has learned how to do acquisitions well. Indeed, finding the right companies to purchase and integrating them into the parent company effectively becomes a critical capability of the parent company.

The business leaders I studied found it much easier to do acquisitions than divestitures. Unfortunately, many companies are very reactive when it comes to divestitures. This is especially the case when it comes to selling off and outsourcing assets. They often find themselves trying to pawn off bad or poorly performing assets, or debt, so they can raise outside money or external capital for themselves. In other words, they arrive very late in the game trying to get rid of poor assets. Because they are somewhat desperate, these companies are tempted to fall into this classic trap: When an asset performs poorly, the first impulse is to get rid of it. Divestitures, for example, often take place typically only after a certain business or business unit has suffered from anemic performance over a number of years.

Figure 8–3 clearly shows that the economy started its downturn in late 2000 when performance started to wane and panic set in. Divestitures, as an annual percentage of total merger, acquisition

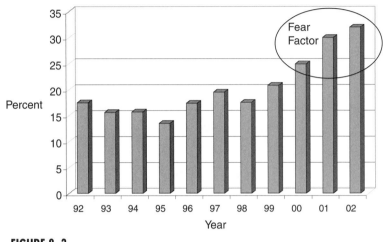

FIGURE 8–3
The fear factor.

and divestiture transactions in the United States, made a large jump upward in 2000, and spiked in 2001 and 2002. And by the look of things currently, this will increase yet again in 2003.

The message here is that companies need to be proactive, not reactive when it comes to divestitures—if they want to avoid business reversals. What these companies should have been doing, of course, was actively paring down their businesses and establishing new growth patterns through mergers and acquisitions. Jack Welch, the former chairman and CEO at GE, set a high standard in the early 1980s when he got rid of a number of businesses that he simply felt were not part of GE's basic strength, that is, its core business.

Welch asserted that he wanted GE businesses to be either number 1 or number 2 in their markets, and anything below that performance would have to go. He encountered grumbling from executives at GE businesses who did not understand what was wrong with being the third or fourth-largest business in their markets. Welch explained that such low-flying businesses lacked the resources to become number 1 or number 2, and therefore he preferred to jettison them at an early stage so that they did not become too great a burden on the overall company. Moreover, GE considered divestitures as part of the overall growth cycle.

Dupont is another company with such discipline. As of May 2003, Dupont was trying to divest its well-known textiles business ($6.5B) even though the business is superior in its space and a strong contributor to the overall business. This is because management believes that the business could create greater shareholder value on its own.

If Welch's GE was the standard for divestitures, Cisco Systems exhibited some signs of being less proactive when it came to paring down its business. It was certainly far from the standard that Welch had set. Although Cisco became well known in the business world as an active and aggressive acquirer, it proved far more reactive on the divestiture side.

As it turns out, it is far easier to be active when it comes to acquisitions as opposed to divestitures. Let's face it: The very act of acquiring has a positive ring to it. Business leaders who roam the business landscape for companies to acquire automatically display characteristics associated with courage, ambition, and zeal—all positive attributes. The CEO who looks at a business unit, a technology asset, or some other segment of his/her company and wants to divest the company of that unit, takes on the attributes of a loser, a failure, someone who has not been able to convert that unit into a high performer. Moreover, the business leader may feel an emotional attachment to the unit; the leader may have personally hired some of the unit's personnel; and certainly, the leader probably signed off on the budgetary allocations that were supposed to help build the unit's success. Getting rid of such an asset can be difficult psychologically, almost like asking a member of the family to stop living at home.

Steve Kaufman has relied on focused corporate transactions to take his company to new levels. In the next chapter, we will study this business leader who excels at the strategy of acquisitions.

THE ACQUISITIVE MAN: THE STEVE KAUFMAN CASE

Remember the stress that has been placed on critical capabilities. One of the overriding differences between leaders who break through the wall and those who don't is a keen focus and intensity on one of those critical capabilities: FOCUSED CORPORATE TRANSACTIONS, OR MERGERS, ACQUISITIONS, AND DIVESTITURES.

Steve Kaufman's Arrow Electronics did not plan systematically to engage in an acquisition strategy. But after he did one acquisition, from that point on, he went from strength to strength.

Before Steve Kaufman took over Arrow Electronics, it was the number 2 player in the industry; earlier, it was only one-third the size of the market leader, Avnet, which had $1 billion in sales. Arrow's market cap was $40 million and sales were only $350 million. Numbers 3, 4, 5, and 6 were between $250–350 million, and were bunched up behind Avnet and Arrow.

Says Kaufman: "No one cared if we lived or died. It was an environment where no one cared outside the company. This was also before the governance and shareholder rights activism, so it was a different era."

No one would have given Arrow a good score as a performer.

Kaufman feels that Arrow's board impeded growth in that period by focusing on performance: "The board is the key determinant in that environment and their appetite for growth or their belief in the strategy of management really drives your ability to sacrifice performance in favor of growth. And that's what Arrow did as a company all through the 1970s, but in the early-to-mid-80s the board became more cautious."

The company had little visibility. Arrow Electronics had hit the wall.

Searching for a Critical Capability

The challenge facing Steve Kaufman was what critical capabilities he might develop and deploy to help Arrow Electronics break through the wall.

Eager to undertake innovation, Steve Kaufman took the company down the GROWTH PATH aggressively. Acquiring the third- and fifth-largest companies in the market, Arrow grew to the size of Avnet. Kaufman "grew" the company to $12 billion in sales by the year 2000. He used acquisitions to help break through the wall.

A word about the business Kaufman is in: The electronic component distribution business started in the 1920s and 1930s, selling radio tubes in lower Manhattan's "Radio Row" on Cortland St., the last vestiges of which vanished in the late 1960s to make way for the construction of the World Trade Center.

By then, many Manhattan distributors had relocated to Long Island or elsewhere, while another breed of distributors formed on the West Coast to sell components to aerospace and defense contractors. Other distributors sprang up in the Midwest to support television manufacturers, and in other locations throughout the United States and Canada to supply computer, telecommunications, consumer, and other original equipment manufacturers (OEMs).

Kaufman joined Arrow in 1982 as president of the Electronics Distribution division, and in 1985, he was appointed president and chief operating officer (COO). In 1986, he succeeded John C. Waddell, one of the company's three principal founders, as CEO, and was elected chairman of the board in 1994.

Prior to joining Arrow, Kaufman served in executive capacities with Midland-Ross Corporation. Previously, he was associated for 10 years with McKinsey & Company, management consultants, where he was a partner from 1976–1980.

From 1982, when Kaufman arrived at Arrow, to 1990, Arrow grew to the size of Avnet and distanced itself from the number 3, 4, and 5 businesses, partially through internal growth, partially through acquiring numbers 3 and 5, and partially through an aggressive overseas acquisition strategy and growth campaign.

When Kaufman took over the leadership of Arrow in 1986, it had $501 million in revenues and a net loss of $31 million. The next year saw some improvement: $562 million in revenue and a shrinking of the loss to just under $10 million.

NEW GROWTH STRATEGY

Kaufman knew that he needed A NEW GROWTH STRATEGY to boost the company's revenues. For him, having the board behind his forward-looking strategy of growth was critical: "We had a board that believed in our strategy. We were essentially invisible to the outside world and therefore we had the luxury of telling the board, 'We're not going to have great performance for the next x years. We have a strategy. Let's monitor our progress on that strategy.' (And we'll be fine.) As long as the board stays firm, the CEO can afford to let performance take a backseat."

The turning point for Arrow Electronics came with its first acquisition: the electronics distribution business of Ducommun Incorporated. The deal was completed on January 12, 1988. In acquiring Ducommun, Arrow was, in fact, acquiring Ducommun's businesses: Kierulff Electronics, Ducommun Data Systems, and MTI Systems. The acquisition was the largest in the history of electronics distribution. The newly combined company would have 1987 sales of $950 million. The purchase made Arrow Electronics the world's largest company engaged exclusively in the distribution of electronic components and related products.

AN ACQUISITIVE MAN

Kaufman used an acquisitions capability to break through the wall, and he never looked back.

It was no small matter to integrate the two companies. It involved not only the relocation and consolidation of 29 sales and warehousing facilities, but also the computer transfer of 350,000 inventory records, 25,000 customer records, 50,000 customer orders, and 25,000 supplier orders.

More acquisitions followed. In the process of these acquisitions, Kaufman began to change the nature of the industry, by getting customers like Intel and Motorola to view Arrow as an important player.

Arrow began to grow by leaps and bounds in 1990. Thanks to its acquisition strategy, Arrow's profits began to grow in the early 1990s: $10.1 million (1990); $8.6 million (1991); $44.8 million (1992); $81.5 million (1993); $111.8 million (1994); $202.5 million (1995); and $202.7 million (1996).

Revenues grew dramatically as well during that six-year period: from $1.542 billion in 1990 to $6.534 billion in 1996.

Intel only paid attention to Arrow when it grew to a certain size.

Kaufman understood very well that only through growth could he keep Arrow a major player. Distribution was getting to be a very large business, and unless one was playing in the $3 billion and up area, it would become very difficult to compete. It appeared that the industry was heading for a consolidation that would leave only four to six distributors remaining.

In 2000, Kaufman said: "In the rest of the world, we're doing acquisitions that fill a hole or gap for us . . . but we don't feel the imperative need to do them. Five, ten years ago, it was a conscious objective strategy to go out and do acquisitions. Now, it's more opportunistic."

Meanwhile, Arrow Electronics expanded its reach in critical markets. In early 2000, it acquired a majority interest in Israeli-based Rapac Electronics, a leading distributor in the electronics field. Tekelec, one of France's leading distributors of high-tech components and systems, joined Arrow in the spring. Its acquisition in mid-2000 of Norway's Jakob Hatteland Electronics, a leader in demand creation and design services, dramatically increased the scope and scale of Arrow's business in the Nordic region.

That same year, Arrow acquired Wyle Electronics in North America and Dicopel in Mexico. The acquisition of Wyle Electronics created an opportunity for Arrow to increase its focus on the networking and communications segments of the industry.

LARGEST DISTRIBUTOR

By 2002, Arrow was one of the world's largest distributors of electronic components and computer products, and a leading provider of services to the electronics industry. Under Kaufman's leadership, Arrow's market capitalization increased from $40 million to more than $4 billion, and the company was listed by *Fortune* magazine as one of the 200 largest public corporations in America. *Fortune* also named Arrow among the most admired corporations in America, and one of the 100 best companies to work for in America. Kaufman had turned the company from a struggling distributor with $500 million in revenues and a huge amount of debt in 1986, into a global leader.

Headquartered in Melville, NY, Arrow served as a supply channel partner for more than 600 suppliers and 200,000 OEMs, contract manufacturers, and commercial customers through more than 225 sales facilities and 23 distribution centers in 39 countries.

Kaufman looks at his own leadership characteristics, the ones that propelled him to the growth side: "I wasn't brilliant; I stumbled into something because I didn't have a choice. I just had the brains to do it again. We did the first acquisition because we were failing." Arrow had lost money for three years in a row (1985, 1986, and 1987); Kaufman didn't get fired, and no one cared. That was 5 percent of sales they lost three years in a row. You cannot exist in a public company doing that. Having done the first acquisition, he had the insight to say, "Let's do it again," and it worked. He brought Arrow from $500m to $13b. He didn't find the acquisition game; he recognized he could play it well after stumbling on to it.

Kaufman talks about the kinds of leadership characteristics that an executive bent on growth and coming from his industry must have. He believes that to have hyper-growth requires a leader who has an innate understanding of either the technology or markets or both that he operates in and is prepared to make major bets based on his gut. The gut comes from being in an industry, technology, or market long enough that you instinctively sense what's possible and plausible.

Growth-oriented leaders are going to avoid seeking the advice of consultants, putting a lot of credence in cash flows, and engaging in projections. They will dismiss the consultants and bean-counters. They are not going to try to put a number on certain products, on whether a lab will make it. They will make certain bets. They will eschew strategic plans on a yearly basis. Such comfortable analysis makes less sense to this leader than making a $1 billion bet based on knowing the business inside and out. This kind of leader gets speed; the more methodical leader loses time grinding out the analysis and can miss the technology window. According to Kaufman, "The hyper-growth guy says, 'I know this will be right.' He may be wrong, but he takes bets that will move his company into new business. Sometimes the growth leader will even be willing to bet the company. A performance guy who was going for the numbers couldn't do that."

But, growth-oriented leaders also know how important the perceptions of their employees and other stakeholders (customers, suppliers, etc.) are to the outcome of any deal. And so, communication becomes essential. Kaufman understood this and made sure that he was constantly in touch with those groups that mattered most to the deals he was putting together. He understood too that he had to have a communication plan in place that included actions and milestones.

When it came time to choosing his replacement, the board picked a performance-oriented executive. It was clear to them that attracting and retaining top talent was crucial for meeting growth targets. According to this view, the business environment was changing, moving from a very unstructured, very high-growth, ambiguous environment to one that required a more disciplined, by-the-numbers management style. "My style wasn't daily, by-the-numbers. We wanted someone with a little less creative flash and a little more by-the-numbers. We didn't want an accountant, a bean-counter. Where I might be viewed as the evangelist or visionary of my industry, working in a very ambiguous world, preparing to make big bets on my gut, because I felt it was right, I wanted a guy who was more prepared to do a little more programmed work. I wanted the guy to keep the ball moving forward steadily, to recognize that now that people who cared who we were, we couldn't be as much risk-taking because it now mattered who we were."

Kaufman and the board understood all too well that the growth environment he had prospered in was running out of speed. With shareholder activism gaining ground and the Arrow board wondering when growth would give way to more of a focus on performance-driven initiatives, they realized that the new leader could not mirror his own leadership style.

At the time, there was a general feeling that shareholders count more. That was an external event over which Arrow had no control. It had started to grow big enough that it appeared on the radar screen as its strategy began to work—and so the company became visible. That caused the board to ask, "When are we going to get performance?" They were talking about performance as profitability.

When the business started, the board asked, "When does *now* come?"

When does Arrow start making the profits in which it had invested strategically for the last eight or nine years? The model shifted: It had played out the acquisition strategy. Then it joined the public market, attaining a $1 billion market cap; people wanted to know when it would start making money.

Once a company is public, it has a different framework. Kaufman was faced with trying to balance the outside world's desire for steady performance with his own intrinsic desire to build a long-term enterprise in the belief that certain investments were required for long-term growth. Things change when you are in the constellation of visible companies. If you're General Motors (GM), you're very, very visible. There's more pressure for steady performance once you're on the radar screen.

Kaufman believes that one problem with U.S. capitalism is that "shareholders' rights" is a strange term. Which shareholders, and for how long? At one point in Arrow's development in the middle of a recession in its cyclical industry, its shareholder base, which had been heavily made up of growth-oriented institutions, was very supportive of its growth strategies. Then it went into a downcycle in the industry. Everyone got hammered because sales and profits went down. The growth investors got out. Value investors bought the shares they sold. Kaufman got four calls from four institutions that had bought 2–3 million of Arrow's shares, and were 15–25 percent of its shareholder base. They wanted to talk with him about his strategies. They thought Arrow was growing too fast and that Kaufman should shrink the company. They said that their models showed that if he shrunk the company, he would generate cash.

They told Kaufman, "[You should] do a massive stock buyback, maybe going private recap. That would boost the stock price short term. The implicit idea: We [the four institutions] will sell and make a lot of money." Those shareholders were with Arrow a maximum of 20–24 months, by which point they were gone. Some made a lot of money. Most made some money. No one lost money. This was in 1996–1997. They were all gone by 1998. Had Kaufman followed their advice or demands as the current share-holders, the company today would be a third of its size, would probably be limping along, or would have been acquired. Had he shrunk the company, he would have given up being in the number 1 and 2 market positions. And Arrow would have lost support of its major suppliers. For Arrow, having Intel and Motorola as suppliers was critical. If he had said he was not growing in order to maximize cash, Intel and Motorola would have found other distributors to grow. His business would have been encumbered dramatically. When those four institutions investors sold, the company would have been weaker.

What did Kaufman tell the four institutions? He told them that their proposal was stupid. But these institutions did have an effect on Arrow. Rather than holding on to cash to improve their balance sheet and pay down debt, Arrow did go out and do a modest stock buyback program. Arrow spent $300 million that reduced its equity by $300 million and increased its debt by $300 million. When the market took off and Arrow started to grow and consume cash and see acquisition opportunities, it was not prevented, but it was modestly hindered. It had a little bit more trouble getting the borrowings it needed to support the growth that was in front of it. Arrow didn't pass on any acquisitions, but it came close to passing on one because it didn't have the cash. The stock buyback did virtually nothing to the stock price at the time. It takes a massive buyback to really affect the price, and what Arrow bought back was only 10–12 percent of stock. It was not enough to move it. Maybe it held the stock up a little bit. Kaufman's view was that the buyback was wasted. It encumbered Arrow's balance sheet, and the company really had to scramble to get cash for a $500 million acquisition when it would have easily had the cash had it not done the buyback.

Kaufman believes that the buyback was 120 percent performance-oriented—performance meaning shareholder value. It improved earnings per share (EPS), but it didn't do anything for its dollar profits; Arrow had used borrowed funds for its buyback.

Kaufman says, "Stock buybacks don't do anything for your ROI. You are sacrificing growth because you're using capital that could have been used for investments."

The long and short of it was that Arrow was moving away from growth initiatives by the late 1990s and Kaufman knew he had to choose a successor reflecting this new reality. What Kaufman and the board were doing—and he knew this—was to take a close look at his leadership characteristics and then say he may have done a great job but that doesn't mean the guy who follows him should be his clone: "The great problems in business succession occur heavily around the unchecked ego and testosterone of the leader who looks in the mirror and sees what he would like his successor to be. There's a problem when you start believing your own press."

The man Arrow chose in the summer of 2000 was Francis Scricco, aged 51, who had joined the company in August 1997 as executive vice president and COO. He was named president in June 1999 and elected to the board of directors in August 1999. He took over as head of the company on July 1, 2000.

Interestingly enough, when Francis Scricco was asked by a journalist how things would differ under his leadership from Kaufman's, he replied, "We have more similarities than differences." He went on to note that both men had roots in Massachusetts; both attended college there; both had worked as consultants; both had worked in industries outside of distribution before joining Arrow; and, the two men had preferred tennis to golf. Finally, Scricco conceded one difference in leadership style: "Steve is more of a visionary. He's capable of developing [a vision] in his head and then laying it down. Me, I'm more likely to throw an idea out in the preliminary stages and let people pick at it. I also tend to be more tenacious on following up on the details. I tend to be more of a list guy."

Scricco finally got it right: What was significant was not that both he and Kaufman preferred tennis or came from Massachusetts. It was that one was a visionary, the other a nuts-and-bolts guy. Arrow's board knew that from the start and that's why they chose Francis Scricco as president and CEO.

Scricco, however, resigned in June 2002. No public explanation was offered for his departure. Daniel W. Duval, a long-time board member, stepped in as Arrow chairman, and served as the interim CEO until February 2003 when William E. Mitchell was named the new president and CEO of Arrow. Duval remained as chairman. Mitchell came to Arrow from Solectron Corp., of San Jose, CA, a leading contract manufacturer, where he served as executive vice president. Mitchell also served as president of Solectron Global Services Inc., a $1.2 billion services outsourcing business.

Just as acquiring new businesses is a critical capability that business executives would be wise to deploy, so too is an ability to change and react to change in the business environment. The next chapter will offer a case study of a business leader who has taken his business from the doldrums to the heights of prosperity by knowing how to change.

CHAPTER 10

THE MERGER MAN: DAN VASELLA BRINGS NOVARTIS TO GREAT SUCCESS

This is the story of how mergers played and may well play a major role in the history of one of the largest pharmaceutical companies, Novartis.

The success of the 1996 merger that created Novartis illustrates how mergers can serve as a CRITICAL CAPABILITY for business leaders as they seek to overcome past business reversals. The possibility—perhaps even the likelihood—that Novartis may grow even larger as the result of future mergers, offers further evidence of the way this critical capability offers value for a company.

The formula for success was not going to be easy. Dan Vasella, the head of Novartis, knew that. He knew all too well that THE TWO FRMS THAT WERE MERGING had stodgy, laid-back cultures. He knew that their business leaders had not been innovative or bold enough.

HITTING THE WALL

Both companies, Ciba-Geigy and Sandoz, had hit walls, though there had been no sudden, precise moment of crisis.

The deal had been arranged on November 30, 1995, when Marc Moret, then chairman of Sandoz, met Ciba-Geigy's chairman, Alex Krauer.

THE MERGER WAS ANNOUNCED on March 7, 1996, and the deal came to $41.2 billion. It was, at the time, the largest industrial merger in history. The new company became the second largest drug maker in the world, holding a 4.4 percent share of the world pharmaceutical market, just behind then-GlaxoWellcome's 4.7 percent; it was twice as large as its nearest rival. The new company had a market cap of $75 billion.

Seven years later, the merger had clearly proven a great success. Novartis is best known to the U.S. drug-consuming population for over-the-counter products such as TheraFlu cold remedies and Maalox antacid. The company has also produced several blockbuster prescription drugs such as Diovan, for hypertension, and Glivec, known in the United States as Gleevec, a cancer breakthrough drug.

Both Ciba-Geigy and Sandoz had been founded in Basel, Switzerland at the end of the 19th Century. By 1996, both were still profitable. Sandoz had business units in pharmaceuticals, nutrition, agribusiness, and chemicals, while Ciba-Geigy had units in healthcare, agriculture, and industrial chemicals.

With the merger, the new company sought a new identity. The chemical businesses were divested. The motto of the new company became "New Skills in the Science of Life." But, the life sciences concept failed, as synergies between pharmaceuticals and agribusiness could not be found. In late 2000, Novartis decided to focus on the more lucrative pharmaceuticals market.

DAN VASELLA'S GOAL WAS FOR NOVARTIS TO BECOME THE WORLD'S LEADER IN SELECTED THERAPEUTIC AREAS. He understood, as he took over the newly merged company, he would have to make swift, daring changes if he wanted to do away with the unproductive aspects of Sandoz and Ciba-Geigy.

He was eager to do just that. He had spent a decent amount of time in the United States and had learned to appreciate the U.S. style of business, with its aggressive emphasis on sales and marketing. He wanted to adopt what he had learned in the United States to his running of the newly merged company. It would take a whole new approach to management. First and foremost, he needed to get Novartis moving; he needed to get it producing high-quality drugs and getting those drugs to market expeditiously. Speed would be of the essence.

At Sandoz, not unlike most pharmaceutical firms at the time, new products required a three-stage process before reaching market: researchers sought out potential drugs; development teams tested and refined them, hoping for regulatory approval; then, marketers peddled the drugs to physicians. Because these steps were undertaken in isolation from one another, the development team would on occasion learn too late that a candidate drug had awful side-effects or that it could not be mass-produced economically; or, the marketing staff learned late in the game that there was not much demand for the new drug they would soon be asked to sell.

Moreover, an excessive amount of command-and-control management at Sandoz inhibited initiative, in Vasella's view. The situation seemed no better at Ciba-Geigy, which was wracked with an epidemic of indecisiveness.

BADLY BEATEN

Risk-averse and slow to produce drugs, Ciba-Geigy and Sandoz were getting beaten badly by their U.S. counterparts. No wonder: The drug pipeline of both firms was essentially dry. When they did have a decent drug, their marketing personnel seemed out of their league. Worst of all, neither company was at all a force in the United States, the largest and freest drug market in the world.

Ciba-Geigy's decision-makers on its executive committee seemed only capable of making compromises. After producing a blockbuster arthritis drug called Voltaren, the company failed to push it in the United States for a full decade after its European debut. Sandoz was no better. Though it had developed a new class of anti-nausea drugs in the late 1980s, its rivals figured out how to gain most of the sales. Part of the blame was a Sandoz culture that had managers working in their offices behind closed doors at a snail's pace. Needless to say, mediocrity was the common standard.

It was not that the scientists at Ciba-Geigy and Sandoz were uncreative; it was simply that no one in either company knew how to get good ideas to market. With no one at the top monitoring them, a lethargic team of scientists conducted too few studies to warrant fast drug approvals. The only hot new drug Novartis had when it came into existence was Diovan for hypertension.

To do away with the snail-like cultures at Ciba-Geigy and Sandoz, Dan Vasella introduced firm performance standards. He hired a whole new breed of highly talented executives and instructed them to keep a focus on the marketing side of the business. He made sure that the right people were properly aligned with the right projects. Perhaps the biggest change was getting rid of the "job for life" commitment that had hovered over the two companies and protected employees. He wanted that protection lifted to make employees work harder. He offered incentives for those who did the hard work.

U.S.-STYLE CAPITALISM

Turning to the U.S. style of capitalism, Vasella enlarged the bonus pool. He developed a stock-option plan. He also pushed Swiss unions to agree to performance-based incentives for everyone, including entry-level workers.

He got rid of managers whom he viewed as complacent (15 of the top 21 posts, as it turned out), and fired 12,500 people in two years from the 134,000-strong Novartis. Accordingly, he was able to increase operating profit margin five points to 24 percent over the same period. Although he initially thought he could reach these results in about a year, he realized that it was simply expecting too much to change the attitude and spirit of such a large company in so short a time.

He introduced a new, dynamic spirit of change that was high-risk and innovative because he knew all too well that changes in the U.S. pharmaceutical industry were helping that country push further and further ahead of European-based pharmaceutical enterprises. He was determined to break through the wall that had been erected by the slothful Ciba-Geigy and Sandoz. To do so, he exhibited a refreshing willingness to change and cope with the changing business environment.

One of the key changes Vasella introduced was a willingness to indulge in HIGH RISK. He was not afraid of making large bets. He was convinced that only such large bets could help Novartis ascend to greatness.

THE MERGER AS A CRITICAL CAPABILITY
Dan Vasella believed that a merger created an opportunity to indulge in high risk, and when confronted with the opportunity, he did not shy away from it.

In 2001, change was indeed in the air: Novartis launched four new drugs, most important of which was Gleevec, a breakthrough cancer pill. It also pioneered programs to improve global access to costly new medicines. Since 2000, it has launched nine groundbreaking drugs—triple its closest rival—and it plans to launch 12 more by 2006. It also acquired a 20 percent stake in its archrival, the Swiss-based Roche Group, Basel's other large drug enterprise. More recently, Novartis announced that it had acquired enough stock in the Roche Group to control 32.7 percent of the voting rights. The announcement made it appear more likely that Dan Vasella would press Roche's founding families to agree to merge Novartis and Roche, creating the world's second-largest pharmaceuticals maker after Pfizer. A Novartis-Roche merger would create a company with yearly sales of $45 billion. Novartis and Roche dominate the market for cancer drugs, organ transplant rejection treatments, and diagnostic testing. The two companies complement each other nicely as well: Novartis has a promising pipeline of new drugs; Roche has a strong sales force to promote those drugs.

Dan Vasella's achievements, which earned him kudos in the media (*BusinessWeek* named him one of the top 25 managers for 2001), did not come easy. Right after the Ciba-Geigy-Sandoz merger, many industry analysts believed that the combined enterprise would produce more harm than good, raising costs and heightening conflicts. Vasella ignored such negative comments, confident that the changes he would introduce would create great new benefits. There was much to do.

Vasella vowed to make major changes in the way the new company did business. It would take risks. It would move faster in producing drugs. Company personnel would be rewarded for delivering. Exhibiting a will to move fast even before Novartis came into existence, Vasella began plans to close plants, consolidate parts of the business, and cut jobs. Sensing a new competitive and dynamic spirit flowing from the top, managers started to work 70-hour weeks to execute. Vasella set a pace: He was often up at 1 a.m. answering e-mails. Once, a colleague suggested he ease up, but Vasella cut the man off, saying he was totally wrong. Rather than ease up, he wanted to increase the pressure even more. And, Vasella watched carefully that he did not waste money on products that were too costly to manufacture.

When Novartis started, it had only one hot drug, Diovan for hypertension. Its only two hits, Sandimmun, or Cyclosporine, for organ transplants (from Sandoz), and Voltaren for arthritis (from Ciba-Geigy), were encountering patent expirations in 1997. So old was the Novartis pipeline that by 1998, over half of its drug sales were from products that had lost patent protection.

Nothing illustrates the pace at which Vasella worked more than the story of Zelnorm, a drug that seemed to him a gem. Some predicted it would become a $1 billion drug, but it had somehow never gotten out of the laboratory. Zelnorm is for indigestion, constipation, stomach pains, and other severe symptoms known as "irritable bowel syndrome" (IBS), for which there were few treatments at the time. As much as 15 percent of the population suffers from such problems, mostly women. The marketing people loved the drug, but clinicians suggested easing off of large-scale trials, doubting whether the syndrome even existed; even if it did, they argued, it would be hard to prove that the drug worked because its symptoms were so subjective.

Most people had lost interest in the drug. Then Dan Vasella came along. He saw the way the staff was trying to bury the drug, but he recalled that he had treated numerous patients who had suffered from the problem when he was a physician. He pushed the trials, then a $100 million decision. And, he promoted a new trials chief, Dr. Jörg Reinhardt, to head of development. Reinhardt was described in one magazine as "a risk-taking sports car enthusiast who likes to zip down the Autobahn at 150 mph." In the past, Novartis marketers had been slow out of the starting gate when a drug was approved; not anymore. It planned a massive TV campaign for Zelnorm.

On July 24, 2002, the Food and Drug Administration (FDA) approved Zelnorm.

By the time he was in the job two years, Vasella believed that he had proven the critics wrong and improved the former companies' value. He noted that the return on net assets had gone from 8.5 percent in 1991 to just fewer than 18 percent in 1997. Shareholder value of Novartis had doubled from $60 billion for Ciba-Geigy and Sandoz just before the merger to $125 billion for Novartis in 1998.

RELYING ON ALIGNMENT

Vasella wanted to create an alignment of interests within the company.

To get from Point A to Point B, an entire company must move toward the same goal. Vasella suggested that alignment was quite important. An organization that was aligned toward common objectives did not have infighting that could tear it apart. From the start, Novartis had focused on what it wanted to be: something different from the past of Ciba-Geigy and Sandoz. Creating something new was a crucial step toward avoiding the battles that were so commonplace in other companies.

One of the major changes Vasella made was to recruit the best leaders. Choosing the right leaders created an environment, he said, that encouraged support and trust while retaining the ambition and self-discipline needed to perform.

He was quite aware of the role he, as business leader, would play. He saw himself, as the CEO, as an agent of change. He had to deal with financial management, but managing scientists and other knowledge workers was also important.

One of Vasella's biggest changes was to modernize the marketing department at Novartis. With far too few resources given to the marketing people, Ciba-Geigy and Sandoz had defaulted that part of the business to the more aggressive, resource-heavy marketing departments of pharmaceutical companies in the United States. Those U.S. firms laid on large television advertising budgets and sent numerous salespeople into the field to see doctors. Vasella hired a new U.S. marketing man, Paulo Costa, who was soon able to increase the Novartis U.S. sales force 50 percent to 4,000; Costa also made sure to focus on the fastest-growing drugs.

To get Novartis employees to work harder, Vasella introduced performance-linked compensation. He put more resources into marketing. Additionally, he increased R&D spending by 46 percent from 1996–2000.

These early moves paid off handsomely. Novartis posted full-year group sales of $19.1 billion for 2001, an increase of 14 percent in local currencies (10 percent in Swiss francs). Pharmaceuticals drove the sales growth, especially in the United States where pharmaceutical sales rose 24 percent. Meanwhile, its rivals—GlaxoSmithKline, Merck, and Bristol-Myers—were suffering from declining revenue growth due to the expiration of patents on their most important drug products. Novartis became the 17th most valuable company in the world; a year earlier, it was 27th.

NOVARTIS BECAME ONE OF THE FASTEST-GROWING MAJOR PHARMACEUTICAL COMPANIES IN THE UNITED STATES. In six short years, it had become one of the world's most admired and energetic pharmaceutical firms. The U.S. contribution to the sales of both the group and pharmaceuticals sectors rose to 43 percent. Net income was $4.181 billion for 2001, an increase of 8 percent.

Novartis products won 15 product approvals around the world, more than any other company in the industry. Investments in R&D climbed to a record 4.2 billion Swiss francs, with the result that by the end of 2001, Novartis had 66 projects in clinical development.

In 2002, Novartis reached sales of $20.9 billion, an 11 percent growth in revenue, and a net income of $4.7 billion, an increase of 4.3 percent. The revenue growth rate was just behind that of two large U.S. competitors, Johnson & Johnson, at 12.3 percent, and Pfizer, at 12 percent. It invested approximately $2.8 billion in R&D.

Unquestionably, Dan Vasella's new high-risk policies were never suited better than in the development of certain high-potential drugs, such as Gleevec, a breakthrough cancer drug. Vasella took the decision to accelerate development in April 1999—against the better judgment of some senior colleagues—after learning of the remarkable early results in only 31 patients who had been enrolled in Phase I trials for the drug. The patients had a rare form of cancer called Cellular Myeloid Leukemia (CML). Vasella told the staff that he did not care what it cost to accelerate the drug's development.

The tiny orange pill had been given to patients who had not been helped by the conventional therapy of Interferon; incredibly, Gleevec worked in all 31 cases.

The number of CML victims in America was relatively small compared to the victims of other forms of cancer. Some 6,650 Americans over the age of 10 are diagnosed with CML each year; worldwide, the figure is 1.3 per 100,000 a year. So while there was an obvious urgency to get the drug in the hands of CML patients, it was not a drug that would make Novartis very much money. But, developing a breakthrough drug of this kind would enhance the reputation of Novartis, and Vasella was well aware of that.

SPEEDING UP DEVELOPMENT

Vasella's decision to go full speed ahead in producing this drug was very high-risk because it increased the costs of failure significantly. His plan was to invest heavily in production up-front, without waiting for the results from further patient trials. Normally, a pharmaceutical company like Novartis would spread the costs and risk of an experimental drug over time, checking how patient trials were doing, making sure that the drug had some merit before investing additional huge sums.

The key to the way Gleevec works is that it is "designed" to target only cancer cells, leaving normal, healthy cells intact. It is, in that sense, a great advance on the most popular form of treatment for CML patients, Interferon, which kills dividing cells with little regard for whether they are cancerous.

Relying on chemotherapy, at best a crude treatment, doctors had been able to slow CML down by killing cancerous cells; but, because the chemotherapy also killed normal cells, cancer patients were left defenseless against the tiniest of maladies. While chemotherapy has the potential to prolong the life of patients, it very often makes patients quite ill. The side-effects in some patients outweigh any benefit.

Gleevec is the first of a new class of drugs called Signal Transduction Inhibitors (STIs), so-called because they interfere with the pathways that signal the growth of cancerous cells. When an STI interrupts a signal transduction pathway, a cell stops dividing, halting the cancer.

Accordingly, with its new mechanism of action proving so successful, Gleevec will surely ignite a great deal more research, encouraging the development of more drugs using its approach.

WINNING FDA APPROVAL

On May 10, 2001, the FDA announced that it had approved Gleevec for distribution in the United States. Speaking at a news conference in Washington, D.C. that day, Dan Vasella noted, "For me personally, this is an especially meaningful occasion. As a physician who has treated many patients, I know what a life-saving drug means for patients who are deathly ill and for their families.

"Speed was an absolute priority for Novartis in developing this drug. Upon the first hint of the dramatic potential of this new agent, Novartis rapidly invested extraordinary manpower to scale up manufacturing and to expedite the clinical development, allowing many, many more patients to enter clinical studies and have access to the drug. We chose to take a significant risk at an early stage, reallocating resources and prioritizing the development of this product. As a result, the new drug application was filed only 32 months after the first dose in man, more than halving the typical drug development time of approximately six years. Based on the dedicated efforts of my Novartis colleagues and a constructive collaboration with the FDA, who granted Gleevec a priority review, we have succeeded in bringing this revolutionary drug to the patients in record time.

"Patient access to Gleevec has been one of our key concerns... and today, we have about 8,000 patients around the world under treatment. We decided to put in place a comprehensive patient assistance program, which insures that uninsured, low-income CML patients are not denied therapy for economic reasons."

First-quarter 2002 sales for Gleevec topped $109 million.

PHYSICIAN TURNED BUSINESSMAN

Dan Vasella came to the business world at a relatively late age. Trained as a physician, he shifted professions in part at least because of a personality that he has described as aggressive, persistent, and ambitious. He had grown weary of the day-to-day routine of seeing patients and was looking for something that was more exciting, more challenging. He felt he would find it in the business world. And so, at the age of 35, he resigned from the hospital where he had been working in Bern, Switzerland, and began working for Sandoz. He was assigned to its U.S. headquarters in East Hanover, NJ.

Asked to do market research, his early days were made difficult by his lack of business experience. But, he had his first big break in 1989, when he spent three months in a management development program at the Harvard Business School. Not only did it provide the necessary tools for him to get ahead in business, but even more important, it enhanced his self-confidence. He now felt that he was as good as any of his peers at Sandoz.

Returning to Sandoz, he was given responsibility for the niche drug Sandostatin, which reduces secretions caused by carcinoid tumors. Expectations for the drug were quite low, but he was determined to make an impact: He and his team provided new uses for treating cancer side effects. Sales grew to $40 million from under $1 million.

He grew to love capitalism. He relished the freedom that businesspeople in the United States had to become successful, contrasting that freedom with the protectionism and government meddling that existed in Europe; in Europe, he found a deep ambivalence toward capitalism.

Remaining in the United States until June 1992, he then became the personal assistant to Rolf Soiron, the new CEO of the pharmaceutical business of Sandoz in Basel, Switzerland. Soiron wanted someone who knew the U.S. market. At first, he worked with the management consulting firm of McKinsey & Company on a six-month analysis of how to reorganize the firm's product development program. He then became global head of product management, a difficult assignment because, while responsible for the bottom line, he had no formal authority over the product heads in various countries.

When Rolf Soiron asked him to become head of development, he worried that he would have trouble with a job that seemed to have less to do with business and more with research. But he managed nicely. He became the COO for six months, and then in 1995, the CEO of Sandoz's pharmaceutical business. When the merger occurred between Sandoz and Ciba-Geigy in December 1996, he was tapped to be the chairman and CEO of the newly merged company. He was 43 years old.

Vasella adopted a leadership style that was decidedly not hands-on. He believed instead that his responsibility as chairman and CEO was to find the best talent, let them do their jobs, and be available when there were large problems to solve. As a result, Vasella introduced a healthy dose of entrepreneurial spirit in the company. Employees began to feel empowered, and felt that they could count on the upper echelons to support their projects, a feeling that was distinctly missing at Ciba-Geigy.

He has been described as a gentleman to a fault, soft-voiced and unimposing; but, many comment as well on his resolve to take risks, to speed up the company's machinery, and to reward those who deliver.

The future of Novartis looks bright. As it contemplated when and how to undertake yet another merger—this one with the Roche group—Novartis was busy strengthening its generics business. It spent $920 million in December 2002 on Lek Pharmaceutical and Chemical of Slovenia, a specialist in manufacturing generic drugs. In January 2003, Lek started selling a generic antibiotic, Amoksiklav, in the United States. In 2002, prior to acquiring Lek, revenue from Novartis' generics business rose 15 percent to $1.8 billion—the only part of the company's business that showed any significant growth. By 2004, it is expected that Novartis will become the number 1 global generics market leader, eclipsing Teva Pharmaceuticals Industries of Israel, which has $2 billion in annual revenue.

Unleashing new drugs for other deadly or debilitating illnesses such as asthma, diabetes, schizophrenia, organ failure, arthritis, skin disorders, and eye disease, and with the Roche Group merger now complete, Novartis has a game plan that aims at producing double-digit growth in the coming years.

CHANGE was the key word in Dan Vasella's case. If he was going to break through the wall, he needed to introduce change into the NEWLY MERGED Novartis. But, the true critical capability that helped the two companies recover from past business reversals was the MERGER itself. To be sure, there are other critical capabilities that business leaders can use to improve their companies' financial pictures. We will examine several of them in the next chapter as we look at one of America's more successful business leaders.

11

MR. PRODUCTIVITY: LARRY BOSSIDY USES INFORMATION TECHNOLOGY TO MOLD A NEW HONEYWELL

We will now look at Larry Bossidy, who for many years cast a giant shadow as the right-hand man to Jack Welch; then, when it became clear that he was too old to succeed Welch, he set off on a second career running a number of major enterprises with great success. With the success that he achieved in his second career post-

GE, he acquired a reputation for knowing how to get things done by applying technology swiftly and effectively.

RUTHLESS EXECUTION

Bossidy is an excellent example of a business leader who used certain CRITICAL CAPABILITIES to energize his company, and in doing so, built an atmosphere where RUTHLESS EXECUTION became the highest value.

Born in Pittsfield, MA, Larry Bossidy is a 1957 graduate of Colgate University with a B.A. in economics. A left-hander with a mean fastball, he was offered a $40,000 signing bonus from the Detroit Tigers, but his mother insisted he go to college. He pitched for Colgate in the College World Series. Even then, he showed a will to win and the energy to succeed. He could be intimidating: As a high-school pitcher, Bossidy dominated the baseball diamond so much that he earned the nickname "Big Boss."

He joined GE as a trainee in 1957. He was COO of GE Credit (now GECS) from 1979–1981, executive vice president and president of GE's Services and Materials sector from 1981–1984, and vice chairman and executive officer of GE from 1984–July 1991. But Bossidy became restless and knew he'd have to look outside GE for further personal growth.

Following his stint at GE, Bossidy was named CEO of AlliedSignal, which merged with Honeywell in 1999 and took its name. Headquartered in Morristown, NJ, the new Honeywell International Inc. is a diversified technology and manufacturing company, serving customers worldwide in the aerospace, automated control systems, automotive, power generation systems, and specialty chemicals industries. Honeywell has 120,000 employees.

AlliedSignal's history dates back to 1920, when Allied Chemical and Dye Corporation was formed as an amalgamation of five U.S. chemical companies; the roots of those five firms date back to the late 1800s. In 1985, Allied Corporation merged with the Signal Companies, Inc. AlliedSignal became a leading advanced technology and manufacturing company and one of the 30 stocks in the Dow Jones industrial average.

Founded in 1885, Honeywell got its start thanks to an innovative device that could adjust the damper of a coal furnace to heat homes more evenly. That product became the world's most popular thermostat, the "Honeywell Round." For over a century, the company's innovations in control technology helped Honeywell gain a reputation for being the world's leading provider of control solutions for buildings, homes, industry, and aerospace.

Larry Bossidy was credited with turning the sleepy manufacturing company of AlliedSignal (circa 1991) into a major internationally diversified aerospace, technology, and manufacturing enterprise, transforming the company nearly a decade later into one of the world's most admired companies. When Larry Bossidy took over AlliedSignal in 1991, the company had revenues of $12.3 billion. He confronted numerous stumbling blocks to progress: 51 separate units (Bossidy liked to refer to them as fiefdoms), each functioning on its own, vying for limited corporate resources. The company faced declining revenues, unchecked capital spending, and excess bureaucracy.

Bossidy was shocked at the LACK OF EXECUTION when he arrived in 1991. Coming from GE, he was accustomed to an organization that got things done, where people met their commitments. He had not expected things to be perfect, but he was not prepared for the malaise that he encountered. Not that the people were not hard-working or bright; they were simply ineffective.

Taking a cue from his former boss, Jack Welch, who urged employees to start every day as if it was their first at work, Bossidy insisted that all employees start to think differently, to change the way they did business, to raise questions about everything. He was determined to bring unity to the place, to integrate those dissimilar businesses.

He proceeded to quintuple the market value of AlliedSignal shares and heavily outperformed the Dow Jones industrial average and Standard & Poor 500 over his tenure. In 1998, he was named CEO of the Year by *Chief Executive* magazine.

When he retired as the head of AlliedSignal in 1999, he had steered the company to 31 consecutive quarters of earnings-per-share growth of 13 percent or more. He had also led the company through an unprecedented period of growth in cash flow. In 2001, free cash flow was $1.4 billion. At the time of the merger with Honeywell in July 1999, AlliedSignal's annual revenues were $15 billion. But due to the merger with Honeywell, the revenues of the newly merged enterprise in 1999 were $23.4 billion a year.

Combining AlliedSignal's and Honeywell's strong aerospace businesses created one of the best known and most valuable franchises in the industry.

MANAGING TALENT

One of the critical capabilities that Bossidy focused on, spending more time on than on any other was MANAGING TALENT.

Larry Bossidy was vigilant in driving his productivity management and talent management strategies. These became important strategies in his running of Honeywell. Only when Bossidy felt that these actions were in place did he feel that Honeywell International HAD EARNED THE RIGHT TO GROW.

One of the more vexing problems Bossidy encountered after joining AlliedSignal was a weakness in the operating management team. Without sufficient bench strength, the company could simply not produce future leaders. When he retired from AlliedSignal, he considered the greatest sign of its strength to be the extraordinary quality of its leadership pipeline. One measure of that quality was that several of the company's senior executives had been recruited to lead other organizations, among them Paul Norris, who became CEO of W. R. Grace, Dan Burnham, hired as Raytheon's CEO, Gregory L. Summe, who became CEO of PerkinElmer, and Frederic M. Poses, who was selected CEO of American Standard.

In June 2002, Bossidy co-authored with Ram Charan a best-selling book called *Execution: The Discipline of Getting Things Done*, detailing his experiences at Honeywell and his business philosophies. I have had the honor of working for Bossidy on a number of occasions in a consulting capacity (which is a rarity, as he is notorious for disliking consultants). In both his book and in watching him, it is clear that he places incredible importance on finding and developing talent.

He clearly makes reference to the fact that he spends a significant portion of his day on talent management. He knew that he had devoted what some thought was an inordinate amount of time and emotional energy to hiring, providing the right experiences for, and developing leaders. He visits the company's plants, meets managers and non-managers alike. It is critical for him to know their capabilities, what they are working on, and how they think about issues.

For the two years following his retirement—1999 and 2000—with Bossidy no longer at the helm, the company lost its execution atmosphere; it failed to deliver results that investors expected and the stock price fell. It seemed like a ship without a rudder. What's more, when GE's plan to acquire (let's not kid ourselves, it was an acquisition) Honeywell unraveled and the company took an enormous hit. Honeywell was so consumed with the integration, it seemed to forget that it had a company to run.

In July 2001, Bossidy was brought in to help get the company back on its feet and deliver results.

DRIVING OUT COSTS

Bossidy's directive from the board was to get the company back in order. So he focused on COST MANAGEMENT: increasing efficiency and developing a consistent commitment to Wall Street that the company would drive out costs and improve cash flow. Bossidy's plan was to try to get the company moving again and appoint a respected successor. All along it was his hope to step down—again—in the summer of 2002. And he did just that.

In his efforts to get Honeywell back on track, Bossidy drove a cost and working capital management program. In 2001, Bossidy came up with a restructuring plan that called for Honeywell, by the end of that year, to take $2.2 billion in charges, mostly to cover the cost of getting rid of 15,800 jobs—13 percent of its workforce—and shut down 51 manufacturing facilities. It was the most ambitious cost-reduction initiative in the history of the company. In Honeywell's crucial aerospace business alone, it was to shed 5,300 people, reducing its ranks by 14 percent to 32,000.

Bossidy also shed under-performers such as the brake-pad unit and turbo-generator business.

THE PUSH FOR SIX SIGMA AND DIGITIZATION

In his drive to push for efficiency and productivity, Bossidy improved cash flow and operating margins, and positioned Honeywell as a global competitive force. For Bossidy, technology served as the main driver to execution discipline. At the core of this drive was six sigma-driven productivity, a favorite Bossidy strategy.

The company's new focus on its six sigma program drove quality and made efficiency improvements. Six sigma's metrics and evaluations became part of each executive's six-month management talent review. Every Honeywell business and function had to include six sigma projects in its yearly operating plans.

Six sigma specialization became a Honeywell standard. Every employee had to be trained as a six sigma "Green Belt," the first level of six sigma expertise. Honeywell produced 100 "Master Black Belts" and "Lean Masters," higher level experts within the company; another 3,000 "Black Belts" and "Lean Experts" were spread throughout the company.

Despite all the fanfare surrounding six sigma, Bossidy came to understand that six sigma alone was insufficient to attain his goals. Accordingly, he decided that in addition to six sigma, digitization (driving emerging information technology throughout key processes) would help create and drive the company's productivity culture. The whole company would eventually be looked at through the lenses of six sigma and digitization.

To make sure that both six sigma and digitization were executed properly, Bossidy brought back talent whom he trusted. One such key figure was Larry Kittelberger, the senior vice president, administrator, and CIO. He had worked with Bossidy in the late 1990s.

From 1994–1999, Kittelberger served as senior vice president and CIO at AlliedSignal, where he established the company's first global communications network, significantly stabilized infrastructure operations, expanded AlliedSignal's electronic commerce capabilities, and directed its global Year 2000 initiative.

In Kittelberger, Bossidy had a loyal leader with a history of delivering results. What is more, Kittelberger also shared a passion for digitization. He truly believed that when done effectively, with focus and commitment, digitization would drive significant and tangible value for the company.

In 2001, Bossidy lured Kittelberger back to Honeywell from a stint at Lucent. Bossidy charged him with organizing the campaign to cut costs and improve the company's overall performance.

Bossidy placed Kittelberger in charge of overseeing the company's digitization efforts—including e-Business—and its worldwide IT organization. Kittelberger also had executive responsibility for Honeywell's global shared services organization. He was, in effect, Bossidy's "Mr. Execution."

Bossidy demanded that the businesses drive efficiencies to re-engineer the company's core processes through the effective use of technology. Bossidy dubbed this his "DIGITIZATION PROGRAM."

Bossidy and Kittelberger believed the company could drive productivity to higher levels. Until then, business units had been making technology decisions independently, not leveraging Honeywell's size or shared services effectively. Kittelberger reorganized the company's technology efforts across its four business units and functional areas (including human resources, legal, finance, and supply chain).

In a digitization kick-off meeting with key executives, Bossidy challenged the company to reach a $500-million direct profit-and-loss (P&L) impact target in three years. To reach that goal, each Honeywell business unit and functional area selected a dedicated digitization team to lead the efforts. It then created an inventory of existing and planned technology initiatives. The next step was to analyze and assess budgetary allocations with the idea of identifying strategic relevance and coming to grips with process efforts. Then, the team outlined key performance indicators and specified metrics to measure the effectiveness of investments. Finally, each business' value chain was deconstructed by major cost drivers, which were used to identify digitization opportunities to provide important financial benefits.

Developing a formal digitization planning process included the creation of digitization scorecards to help each business unit monitor and manage investments. It also included assigning a digitization champion who would be accountable for driving success within each business unit and function. Finally, it included developing awareness of the value of digital strategies and "ownership" at the business unit and president levels.

The business units developed leading practices in technology portfolio management, including the development of short-term financial and operational targets and the creation of quantitative measures to monitor results at both the department and corporate levels. In many cases, this meant redesigning financial measurement systems to align business strategies with technology investing and creating a corporate reward system tied to digitization.

TO TRACK THEIR PROGRESS, A WEB-BASED SOLUTION WAS BUILT, WHERE ALL DIGITIZATION WAS TRACKED. IT PROVIDED THE COMPANY WITH A MONTHLY SCORECARD TO VALIDATE SAVINGS AND OTHER BENEFTS ON PROJECTS.

Both six sigma and digitization had a positive effect on Honeywell's customers and supply chains. Integrated into one function were materials production planning, just-in-time inventory scheduling, delivery commitments, real-time collaborative design, and six sigma tools. Bossidy found that it made the entire customer/supplier process chain transparent and immediately adaptable.

Results came quickly: Within one calendar year, Honeywell had achieved over $300 million in direct cost savings. It had reached 60 percent of its three-year goal within one year, with a total productivity improvement of $1.3 billion. It expected to reach its $500-million target in 2003, one year ahead of schedule. These numbers were the results of a culture with improved focus and sense of purpose.

In the summer of 2002, Larry Bossidy stepped down as the head of Honeywell International. Thanks to his major programs to improve the quality and efficiency of the company he led, he secured a solid place for himself as one of the great business figures of the era.

In the final chapter, we focus our thinking on summarizing the key practices required to break through the wall. The Ruthless Execution Index is a guide to help identify those practices required in your organization.

V

WHAT IT ALL MEANS

12

Final Thoughts

Hitting the wall *has* become a new business norm, and with economic conditions as they are today, business reversals haunt the leadership of more and more companies. This book has tried to offer urgent guidance on how to return to the path of success, on how businesses can recover after HITTING PERFORMANCE

WALLS. My hope is that after reading this book, you feel that it is possible to revitalize your organization, and that you have some key principles and tools to do so.

As this book shows, many of the biggest companies in the business world have hit the wall, and some of their leaders have figured out how to reorganize their companies for comebacks. These successful leaders are highlighted in this book because they have experienced breaking through the wall, or as in the case of Cisco, are in the process of trying to do so.

It's never easy to provide a roadmap for business recovery. But, it is possible, as demonstrated in these pages, to identify successful practices of key business leaders.

If you take anything away from this book, it should be this: Leaders who pull themselves through various setbacks demonstrate common behavior patterns summed up neatly by the phrase *ruthless execution.*

Jack Welch believed that developing a business philosophy was one of the best way to build focus and purpose as he sought to steer GE toward new heights. John Chambers sensed a need to strategically recalibrate as a means to steer Cisco Systems through the technology collapse of 2000–2003. Shifting gears toward more performance-oriented initiatives to stabilize its core business is positioning Cisco well to break through its wall.

Lou Gerstner had faith that the products and processes that were part of IBM were perfectly adequate; but, the company required someone to impose discipline throughout the ranks, and once he did that, he helped IBM break through the wall.

You've been given a great deal of information to process in these pages. A key point to remember is that there is a logical sequence to the various strategies elaborated on and a set of common themes that link all of these strategies together.

As noted in Chapter 1, business leaders who have successfully broken through the wall drive through a sequence that roughly follows the order of this book:

- RECALIBRATE YOUR STRATEGIES (LEADERSHIP)

- RECALIBRATE YOUR RULES (GOVERNANCE)

- RECALIBRATE YOUR BUSINESS (CRITICAL CAPABILITIES)

The very first step that business leaders should take in attempting to reverse a business setback is to recalibrate their strategies. They must rearrange the portfolio of business initiatives, assess how resources are being allocated to various initiatives, and set a course for the direction that the company should take. At this stage, these leaders operate within the leadership framework as they decide what it is they must recalibrate. Building and institutionalizing a business philosophy facilitates that process.

Setting a new strategic course requires strong analytical capabilities. It requires carefully, but swiftly, examining strategic options in a rigorous and thorough manner, and learning what truly matters in the marketplace.

Next, having learned what it is they want to do, business leaders must figure out how to do it. In effect, they need to recalibrate key governance elements and establish new rules of the game. They must establish processes that drive accountability and discipline to focus on what matters. To that end, there should be a clear focus on results, for that is the only thing that matters to these leaders. The system they put in place emphasizes that. Explaining away unfavorable results is not an option for them.

Finally, these leaders are ready to put recalibration into action. They need to develop certain critical capabilities that are, in and of themselves, the very essence of recalibrating. As noted earlier, these leaders actively engage in critical capabilities such as vigilant productivity management, talent management, and focused-corporate transactions. Through these critical capabilities, business leaders recalibrate their businesses in search of driving better performance platforms.

I strongly advise following the logical sequence mentioned above. In other words, it makes more sense to recalibrate various strategies *before* attempting to establish the rules of the game; and, it makes more sense to establish the rules of the game before recalibrating execution (before activating one or more critical capabilities).

This is not to say that you must begin governance-like activity only after you have recalibrated various strategies. Certainly these strategies can and often do occur at the same time. It is, however, difficult and less effective to focus on the next step without having a strong base from which to work.

The bottom line is that business leaders need not change what they are about, need not alter their personalities. Rather, they must change what they do and what they focus on. The business leaders highlighted in this book have various personas. Some are great public speakers, outwardly forceful and aggressive; others are more laid-back, shy, and retiring types. Perhaps the most charismatic of the leaders described is Cisco Systems' John Chambers. But, I certainly never meant to suggest that in bad times, Chambers would benefit by being a little bit less charismatic. By no means would I ever suggest that he tone down his "salesmanship." Indeed, the leadership ingredients required to break through any wall are divorced from such personality traits. Those ingredients simply require business leaders to be profoundly objective and straightforward, and deal with a company's options, the rules of the game, and required actions. The point here is that all leaders and change agents can benefit from adopting these leadership ingredients, whether they are leaders of a business, functional area, or any organization.

One final thought: You will by now have realized that this book has addressed one of the profound business issues of today: how to effect change within an organization. The book talks about a particular kind of change, one that is required of business leaders whose companies are experiencing business reversals. To recover from such reversals, these leaders have to change their companies. This book provides a roadmap for doing just that.

Even at this late stage of the book, you may be asking: How can I know whether my company, more than other companies, needs to pursue these prescriptions? Simply ask yourself whether your organization has been under-performing relative to its peer group for a significant period of time (at least one year); and then ask yourself whether your organization has tried to close these performance gaps. If the answer to either question is "Yes," you have every reason to believe that you will benefit by putting the ideas behind *Ruthless Execution* into practice.

As mentioned throughout the book, companies go through ups and downs and typically will experience performance plateaus or even hitting the wall on more than one occasion. UNFORTU-NATELY, MOST TRANSFORMATION EFFORTS START FAST BUT CAN PETER OUT OVER TIME, USUALLY AT ABOUT THE TWO-YEAR MARK. It is at this point that most companies find themselves going through the motions and complacency sets in. Don't get me wrong, I've found that most companies continue to measure their transformation "activities," but they are no longer measuring for results that matter. They are on autopilot. It is imperative that you are always keeping an eye out for the signals and perform reassessment on a regular basis. THE PRACTICES WE TALK ABOUT IN THIS BOOK MUST BECOME PART OF THE CORPORATE DNA AND NOT MERELY ONE-TIME EVENTS.

I have laid out numerous practices that are key to breaking through the wall (examples: working capital management and portfolio management discipline). To break through a wall, it's not necessary to employ every single one of these practices. It's really up to you to pick and choose which of these seem the most appropriate as you wrestle with your own specific set of business dilemmas.

The question remains: How can you figure out which of these strategies to use?

To help you with that, I have developed a Ruthless Execution Index. It is a list of statements to help gauge the extent to which your organization ruthlessly executes. These statements offer "signposts," or if you will, "red flags," that you need to watch out for in your business.

Ruthless Execution Index

Instructions for using the Ruthless Execution Index:

1. In Table 12–1, you will find 54 statements on the left-hand side of the Index.

2. Go through the list of statements and circle the number that best corresponds to your level of agreement with each statement (Disagree = 0; Somewhat agree = 1; Strongly agree = 2).

3. Add up the numbers:

   If you score between 0 and 35, you are far from ruthless execution and have significant risks in your organization.

   If you score between 35 and 72, you have good execution practices, but have some gaps to close.

   If you score above 72, you are ruthlessly executing.

TABLE 12–1   Ruthless Execution Index

	STATEMENTS	DISAGREE	SOMEWHAT AGREE	STRONGLY AGREE
LEADERSHIP				
1	My company clearly understands which customers are most profitable and why.	0	1	2
2	We have detailed knowledge of what creates value for our customers.	0	1	2
3	We know what share of that value we capture.	0	1	2
4	Our company is relentless about ensuring a direct linkage of initiatives to strategic imperatives.	0	1	2
5	Our company's key "battlefields" are clearly communicated and well-understood across the organization.	0	1	2
6	We are spending the right amount in the right areas.	0	1	2
7	Our company effectively balances between short-term performance and longer term growth investments.	0	1	2
8	Our investment/project selection process requires business leaders to allocate total costs and benefits to their P&L statements.	0	1	2
9	We have a planning and review rhythm (quarterly milestones).	0	1	2
10	Our investment decisions are based on sound analytical rigor.	0	1	2

TABLE 12–1 Ruthless Execution Index (Continued)

	STATEMENTS	DISAGREE	SOMEWHAT AGREE	STRONGLY AGREE
11	We effectively analyze and prioritize initiatives/investments.	0	1	2
12	Our company has a consistent and thorough mechanism for assessing and selecting investments and projects.	0	1	2
13	Our company has a process for revising investment and project priorities throughout the year.	0	1	2
14	Our company has good visibility into the total costs and benefits of its investments.	0	1	2
15	The majority of our capital expenses and employees are focused on strategic investments and projects.	0	1	2
GOVERNANCE				
16	We have across-the-board buy-in and compliance for investment selection criteria from all senior leadership.	0	1	2
17	The senior-most leaders of our company are actively involved in the prioritization and review of initiatives.	0	1	2
18	We validate and measure our strategies in a rigorous and fact-based manner.	0	1	2
19	Our company clearly links incentives and rewards to results not activities.	0	1	2

TABLE 12–1 Ruthless Execution Index (Continued)

	STATEMENTS	DISAGREE	SOMEWHAT AGREE	STRONGLY AGREE
20	Our company regularly performs post-implementation audits of initiatives to assess actual costs and benefits.	0	1	2
21	Our company has good visibility into 90 percent of the projects and initiatives across the entire enterprise.	0	1	2
22	Our capital management process can identify and eliminate sandbagging and other budget games.	0	1	2
23	Our company can easily address mid-term funding or reallocation requests when an appropriate opportunity presents itself.	0	1	2
24	Our company has established a common lexicon and set of standards by which investment decisions get made.	0	1	2
25	Our company has an effective method for identifying and funding cross-functional initiatives?	0	1	2
26	Our company has a high compliance rate as it relates to following decision-making standards.	0	1	2
27	Our company has a culture of discipline and rigor.	0	1	2

TABLE 12–1   Ruthless Execution Index (Continued)

	STATEMENTS	DISAGREE	SOMEWHAT AGREE	STRONGLY AGREE
28	Our company has an effective process for allocating resources to strategic investments.	0	1	2
29	Our company focuses on less than five performance measures by which results get judged.	0	1	2
30	We revisit and recalibrate our operating measures every two years.	0	1	2
31	Our company revisits and recalibrates its operating budget on a quarterly basis.	0	1	2
32	Performance measures are applied consistently and fairly across all investments.	0	1	2
33	Our company's performance measures are easily understood by the troops and are relevant to their daily activities.	0	1	2
34	Our company sets "stretch goals" that are fact-based and defendable.	0	1	2
35	Our company has the technical tools to effectively prioritize investments and track performance.	0	1	2
36	We kill/close non-performing initiatives on a regular basis.	0	1	2

TABLE 12–1 Ruthless Execution Index (Continued)

	STATEMENTS	DISAGREE	SOMEWHAT AGREE	STRONGLY AGREE
CRITICAL CAPABILITIES				
37	Our company effectively and regularly manages costs and productivity. It's in our DNA.	0	1	2
38	We have cost management institutionalized throughout the organization.	0	1	2
39	Our people understand and effectively manage working capital.	0	1	2
40	Our leadership team is IT-smart.	0	1	2
41	Our IT investments clearly drive measurable value for the company.	0	1	2
42	Our cost performance is better than our peer group's.	0	1	2
43	We have a proactive and disciplined approach of identifying and assessing potential acquisitions.	0	1	2
44	Our company actively and consistently assesses opportunities for timely divestitures.	0	1	2
45	We focus our acquisition efforts to drive growth.	0	1	2
46	We have a process that requires and ensures that projects deliver on key milestones every three months.	0	1	2

TABLE 12–1   Ruthless Execution Index (Continued)

	STATEMENTS	DISAGREE	SOMEWHAT AGREE	STRONGLY AGREE
47	Our company has a fine-tuned integration process for acquisitions.	0	1	2
48	Our corporate center is adding distinctive value to each business unit.	0	1	2
49	We are consistently developing talent at all levels of the organization.	0	1	2
50	We put an emphasis on keeping the talent needed for growth.	0	1	2
51	Our company ensures that top talent gets allocated to strategic projects.	0	1	2
52	In our company, non-performers cannot survive for longer than twelve months. We have a process for identifying and eliminating dead wood.	0	1	2
53	Our leaders have deep succession plans.	0	1	2
54	Our senior leadership spends one day per week finding and developing new talent.	0	1	2
TOTAL SCORE:				

INDEX

A

accountability systems, 18–19, 96–99
acquisitions
    example, Arrow Electronics' Steve Kaufman
        growth strategies, 168–170, 174–175
        leadership characteristics, 171–172
        market position, 170–171
        overview, 165–168
        shareholders' rights, 173
        successors to Kaufman, 175–176
    focused corporate transactions, 157–164
alignment, 98
    business philosophies, 135

B

bankruptcies, 5–6
Baxter International's Harry Kraemer, example business philosophies
    alignment, 135
    fixation on expectations, 135–138
    goals, short and long term, 140–142
    overview, 131–135
    Shared Investment Plan, 137–138
    strategic bywords, 138–140
Bossidy, Larry (Honeywell), example of information technology-driven business
    Bossidy's background, 194–198
    cost management, 198
    digitization, 200–202
    overview, 193–198
    six sigma, 199–200, 202
breakthrough strategies, performance portfolio framework, 36, 38, 43, 103, 106–107
business philosophies, 16–17
    basics, 48–50
    communication, consistency, 52
    communication, rules, 51–52
    definition, 48
    example, Baxter International's Harry Kraemer
        alignment, 135
        fixation on expectations, 135–138
        goals, short and long term, 140–142
        overview, 131–135
        Shared Investment Plan, 137–138
        strategic bywords, 138–140
    example, General Electric's Jack Welch
        communication of ideas, 60–61

"learning culture," 63–64
Number 2, Number 2 strategy, 55–56
overview, 53–55
six sigma, 64, 65–67
"stretch," 62–63
values list, 67–69
Welch's "quantum leap," 58–60
"work out," 62–65
business reversals
figuring out causes, 9–10
strategies to counteract
run-and-gun, 11–12
ruthless execution, 12–13
slash-and-burn, 12–13
businesses
bankruptcies, 5–6
fewer worries for leaders, 6–8
hitting the wall, 5–6
need for ruthless execution
strategies, 4, 10–11
scandals, 13

C

capital investments, 108–109
Ciba-Geigy, 180–181
Cisco Systems' John Chambers,
example of strategic
calibration
Cisco primed for growth before
Chambers, 78–80
economy
recovery signs, 90–92
weakened state, 86–90
"healthy paranoia," 77–78
most valuable U.S. company, 75–77
overview, 71–74
purchase of Crescendo, 80–85
Collins, Jim, 110
communication in business
philosophies
aspect of consistency, 138–141
consistency, 52, 98–99

example, Baxter International's
Harry Kraemer, 138–141
example, General Electric's Jack
Welch, 60–61
rules, 51–52
constructive impatience, 123–124
cost management, 147–149
information technology-driven
business, 198
credibility, aspect of consistency, 138–141
Crescendo purchase by Cisco Systems, 80–85
critical capabilities, 15, 207
basics, 146–147
focused corporate transactions, 22–23, 157–160
acquisitions, 160–164
example, Arrow Electronics'
Steve Kaufman, 165–176
mergers, example, Novartis's
Dan Vasella, 177–192
productivity management, 21–22
basics, 147
cost management, 147–149
information technology-driven
improvements, 150–152
information technology-driven
improvements, example,
Honeywell's Larry
Bossidy, 193–205
working capital management, 149–150
ruthless execution checklist, 145–146
Ruthless Execution Index, 215–216
talent management, 22
basics, 152–154
bringing on the best, 155–157

D

digitization, information technology-driven business, 200–202
discipline, 19–21, 107–108

aspect of consistency, 138–141
capital investments, 108–109
consistency of leaders, 110–112
example, IBM's Lou Gerstner
    constructive impatience, 123–
      124
    overview, 113–115
    preventing breakup, 119–121
    realistic goals, 125–126
    stress on not staying behind
      desk, 127–129
    stress on services, 126–127
example, Jim Collins, 110
divestitures, 159
Drucker, Peter, 8

F

focus, aspect of consistency, 138–141
"focus and execution" (Cisco Systems),
    87
focused corporate transactions, 157–
    160
    acquisitions, 160–164
    divestitures, 159
    example, Arrow Electronics' Steve
      Kaufman
      growth strategies, 168–170,
        174–175
      leadership characteristics,
        171–172
      market position, 170–171
      overview, 165–168
      shareholders' rights, 173
      successors to Kaufman, 175–
        176
fundamentals (new), performance
    portfolio framework, 36–
    37, 43, 103, 106–107

G

General Electric's Jack Welch
    example of business philosophies
      communication of ideas, 60–
        61

"learning culture," 63–64
    Number 2, Number 2 strategy,
      55–56
    overview, 53–55
    six sigma, 64, 65–67
    "stretch," 62–63
    values list, 67–69
    Welch's "quantum leap," 58–
      60
    "work out," 62–65
Gerstner, Lou (IBM), example of
    discipline
    constructive impatience, 123–124
    emphasis
      on not staying behind desk,
        127–129
      on services, 126–127
    overview, 113–115
    position under John Akers
      decline, 117–119
      decline, reasons, 121–122
      leading computer company,
        115–117
    preventing breakup, 119–121
    realistic goals, 125–126
*Good to Great, Why Some Companies
    Make the Leap. . . and
    Others Don't* (Collins),
    111
governance, 15, 207
    accountability, 18–19, 96–99
    commitment, 97, 99, 112
    compliance, 112
    discipline, 19–21, 107–108
      capital investments, 108–109
      consistency of leaders, 110–
        112
      example, IBM's Lou Gerstner,
        113–129
    performance management
      systems, 19, 100–101
    measurements, 101–107
    performance portfolio framework,
      103, 107
    rigor, 19, 104–108

ruthless execution checklist, 95–96
Ruthless Execution Index, 212–214
growth engines, Cisco Systems, 73, 75–77
balance between growth and performance, 84
primed for growth, 78–80

H

"healthy paranoia," 77–78
hitting the wall
Cisco Systems, 72
definition, 5–6
ruthless execution strategies, 205–210
Honeywell's Larry Bossidy, example of information technology-driven business
Bossidy's background, 194–198
cost management, 198
digitization, 200–202
overview, 193–198
six sigma, 199–200, 202

I

IBM's Lou Gerstner, example of discipline
constructive impatience, 123–124
emphasis
on not staying behind desk, 127–129
on services, 126–127
overview, 113–115
position under John Akers
decline, 117–119
decline, reasons, 121–122
leading computer company, 115–117
preventing breakup, 119–121
realistic goals, 125–126
information technology-driven business, 150–152

example, Honeywell's Larry Bossidy
Bossidy's background, 194–198
cost management, 198
digitization, 200–202
overview, 193–198
six sigma, 199–200, 202

K

Kaufman, Steve (Arrow Electronics), example of focused corporate transactions
growth strategies, 168–170, 174–175
leadership characteristics, 171–172
market position, 170–171
overview, 165–168
shareholders' rights, 173
successors to Kaufman, 175–176
Kittelberger, Larry, 199–200
Kraemer, Harry (Baxter International), example of business philosophies
alignment, 135
fixation on expectations, 135–138
goals, short and long term, 140–142
overview, 131–135
Shared Investment Plan, 137–138
strategic bywords, 138–140

L

leadership, 15–16, 207
business philosophies, 16–17
basics, 48–50
communication, consistency, 52
communication, rules, 51–52
definition, 48
example, Baxter International's Harry Kraemer, 131–142

example, General Electric's Jack Welch, 53–69
characteristics for focused corporate transactions, 171–172
ruthless execution checklist, 28
Ruthless Execution Index, 211–212
strategic recalibration, 16, 28–29
core revitalization, 29–30
example, Cisco Systems' John Chambers, 71–92
guidelines, 38–40
performance portfolio framework, 34–38
portfolio traps, 46–47
portfolios of initiatives, 30–33
reading environments, 33
rules, 42
"learning culture," 63–64

M

mergers
example, Arrow Electronics' Steve Kaufman
growth strategies, 168–170, 174–175
leadership characteristics, 171–172
market position, 170–171
overview, 165–168
shareholders' rights, 173
successors to Kaufman, 175–176
example, Novartis's Dan Vasella
FDA approval of new drugs, 188–189
history of Ciba-Geigy and Sandoz, 180–181
implementing U.S. style of capitalism, 181–187
overview, 177–180
speeding up development, 187–188
Vasella's background, 189–192

N

Novartis's Dan Vasella, example of successful mergers
FDA approval of new drugs, 188–189
history of Ciba-Geigy and Sandoz, 180–181
implementing U.S. style of capitalism, 181–187
overview, 177–180
speeding up development, 187–188
Vasella's background, 189–192
Number 2, Number 2 strategy, 55–56

O

operational excellence in performance portfolio framework, 36–37, 43, 103, 106–107

P

performance management systems, 19, 100–101
measurements, 101–107
performance portfolio framework, 34–38, 103, 107
breakthroughs, 36, 38, 43
management rules, 40–46
new fundamentals, 36–37, 43
operational excellence, 36–37, 43
portfolio traps, 46–47
portfolios of initiatives, 30–33
rational experiments, 36–38, 43
personnel, talent management, 88
basics, 152–154
Cisco Systems, 88
bringing on the best, 155–157
philosophies for business, 16–17
basics, 48–50
communication, consistency, 52
communication, rules, 51–52
definition, 48
example, Baxter International's Harry Kraemer
alignment, 135

fixation on expectations, 135–
138
goals, short and long term,
140–142
overview, 131–135
Shared Investment Plan, 137–
138
strategic bywords, 138–140
example, General Electric's Jack
Welch
communication of ideas, 60–
61
"learning culture," 63–64
Number 2, Number 2 strategy,
55–56
overview, 53–55
six sigma, 64, 65–67
"stretch," 62–63
values list, 67–69
Welch's "quantum leap," 58–
60
"work out," 62–65
portfolio framework. *See* performance
portfolio framework
productivity management, 21
basics, 147
cost management, 147–149
information technology-driven
improvements, 150–152
example, Honeywell's Larry
Bossidy, 193–205
principles of, 152
working capital management, 149–
150

Q

"quantum leap" (GE), 58–60

R

rational experiments, performance
portfolio framework, 36–
38, 43, 103, 106–107
run-and-gun strategy *versus* other
strategies, 11–13

ruthless execution
counteracting business reversals,
12–14
governance, 15, 18–21, 207
checklist, 95–96
leadership, 15–17, 207
checklist, 28
origin of term, 3–4
Ruthless Execution Index
critical capabilities, 215–216
checklist, 145–146
governance, 212–214
instructions for using, 207,
210
leadership, 211–212
strategies
after hitting the wall,
summary, 205–210
need for, 4

S

Sandoz, 180–181
Shared Investment Plan (Baxter
International), 137–138
shareholders' rights, 173
six sigma
General Electric, 64, 65–67
Honeywell, 199–200, 202
slash-and-burn strategy *versus* other
strategies, 12–13
strategic recalibration, 28–29
basics, 16
core revitalization, 29–30
definition, 15
example, Cisco Systems' John
Chambers
Cisco primed for growth
before Chambers, 78–80
economy, recovery signs, 90–
92
economy, weakened, 86–90
"heavy paranoia," 77–78
most valuable U.S. company,
75–77
overview, 71–74

purchase of Crescendo, 80–85
guidelines, 38–40
performance portfolio framework,
34–38
portfolio traps, 46–47
portfolios of initiatives, 30–33
reading environments, 33
"stretch" (GE), 62–63

T

talent management
basics, 152–154
Cisco Systems, 88
bringing on the best, 155–157

V

values list (GE), 67–69
Vasella, Dan (Novartis), example of
successful mergers
FDA approval of new drugs, 188–
189

history of Ciba-Geigy and Sandoz,
180–181
implementing U.S. style of
capitalism, 181–187
overview, 177–180
speeding up development, 187–188
Vasella's background, 189–192

W

Welch, Jack (General Electric),
example of business
philosophies
communication of ideas, 60–61
"learning culture," 63–64
Number 2, Number 2 strategy, 55–
56
overview, 53–55
six sigma, 64, 65–67
"stretch," 62–63
values list, 67–69
Welch's "quantum leap," 58–60
"work out," 62–65
working capital management, 149–150

8 reasons why you should read the Financial Times for 4 weeks RISK-FREE!

To help you stay current with significant
developments in the world economy ...
and to assist you to make informed business
decisions — the Financial Times brings you:

 Fast, meaningful overviews of international affairs ... plus daily briefings on major world news.

 Perceptive coverage of economic, business, financial and political developments with special focus on emerging markets.

 More international business news than any other publication.

 Sophisticated financial analysis and commentary on world market activity plus stock quotes from over 30 countries.

 Reports on international companies and a section on global investing.

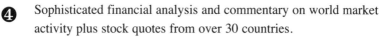 Specialized pages on management, marketing, advertising and technological innovations from all parts of the world.

 Highly valued single-topic special reports (over 200 annually) on countries, industries, investment opportunities, technology and more.

The Saturday Weekend FT section — a globetrotter's guide to
leisure-time activities around the world: the arts, fine dining, travel,
sports and more.

FT FINANCIAL TIMES
World business newspaper